Emma Dorothy Eliza Nevitte Southworth

Sybil Brotherton

Emma Dorothy Eliza Nevitte Southworth

Sybil Brotherton

ISBN/EAN: 9783337346416

Printed in Europe, USA, Canada, Australia, Japan

Cover: Foto ©Thomas Meinert / pixelio.de

More available books at **www.hansebooks.com**

SYBIL BROTHERTON.

A NOVEL.

BY MRS. EMMA D. E. N. SOUTHWORTH.
AUTHOR OF "SELF-MADE," "FAIR PLAY," "THE MISSING BRIDE,"
"ISHMAEL," "HOW HE WON HER," "THE DESERTED WIFE,"
"THE LOST HEIRESS," "SELF-RAISED," ETC.

Mrs. Southworth is a woman of brilliant genius, is one of the most original and talented of living female writers, and is by all odds the best writer of fiction in this country, for she has no superior. Her style is forcible and bold, and there is a chasteness and purity in all she writes, which commend her works to the approbation of every thoughtful mind. There is an exciting interest throughout all her compositions, which renders them the most popular novels in the English language.

PHILADELPHIA:
T. B. PETERSON & BROTHERS;
306 CHESTNUT STREET.

COPYRIGHT:
T. B. PETERSON & BROTHERS.
1879.

CONTENTS.

Chapter.		Page
I.	THE HOMESTEAD — THE FAMILY	21
II.	THE MESSENGER — THE NOVEL READERS.	27
III.	THE BALL AND THE BEAUX	37
IV.	"MY GRANDFATHER, LORD MAINWARING."	47
V.	THE YOUNG WIFE	52
VI.	THE YOUNG MOTHER	59
VII.	KATY'S MISHAPS IN THE CITY	72
VIII.	THE CAPTAIN'S NEWS	81
IX.	GENERAL BUSHROD BROTHERTON	92
X.	THE PASTOR	106
XI.	SYBIL A WIDOW	117
XII.	GENERAL AND MRS. BROTHERTON	120
XIII.	SYBIL'S DREAM OF HAPPINESS	129
XIV.	THE AWAKENING	133
XV.	THE STRUGGLE	157

SYBIL BROTHERTON.
A NOVEL.
BY MRS. EMMA D. E. N. SOUTHWORTH.
AUTHOR OF "ISHMAEL," "SELF-RAISED," ETC.

CHAPTER I.

THE HOMESTEAD — THE FAMILY.

IN one of the lower counties of Maryland, and in one of the first settled neighborhoods, surrounded by forest-crowned hills, and embosomed in trees, stood the mansion of the Brotherton family. It was a queer, old-fashioned house, with many gable ends, and a very steep roof, and windows of diamond-shaped panes set in lead sashes. These sashes, with the bricks of which the house was built, had been imported from "the old country."

It was the pride of the Brotherton family that they had come over with Lord Baltimore; but whether as friend or footman to his lordship, tradition saith not. I can go no further back than Hurbert Brotherton, who flourished about a hundred years ago. He was a notorious fox-hunter, and a celebrated *bon vivant* in general; gave great hunts, great dinners, and great balls, and discovered a great talent for the manufacturing of wings wherewith his acres might fly away. His wings "worked extremely well," as inventors and patentees say, so well that Hubert Brotherton, who at twenty-one could stand upon the highest point in his native county, and looking around call all the land in sight his own, died at forty, a poor man. It is a good illustration of the vicissitudes of life, the fact that the descendants of Hubert Brotherton, who in 1747 owned nearly a quarter part of the whole State of Maryland, do not now possess a foot of land in any country; and that the children of James Howlet, a domestic of the Brotherton family, have risen to the highest places in the army, the navy, and the senate; but then the former sunk through idleness, sensuality, and extravagance; the latter rose by energy, industry, and sobriety.

Brotherton Hall had been some years in chancery at the time our story commences. The sole representatives of the Brotherton family were, now, Mrs. Judith Brotherton and her granddaughter Sybil. That dear old lady was a character! Heaven bless her! I fear I shall caricature the portrait in trying to portray her excellent, but somewhat complex nature. Just as when I was a little girl, and would have some beautiful ideal face haunting my imagination, and, taking a pencil to draw it, would produce some hideous monstrosity, and throw away pencil and sketch in disgust.

Mrs. Brotherton had been very handsome in her youth, and was still a fine-looking old lady. She had a tall, stately figure, with singularly small feet and hands. Her high forehead and small Roman nose were relieved from hauteur by the tender expression of her deep-blue eyes, and the beautiful contour of her mouth. Now don't sneer, young ladies and gentlemen; I have seen both old men and old women with very beautiful and attractive faces, albeit somewhat gray and wrinkled, and, when I was a school girl, I was very near falling in love with an old gentleman of sixty, for his beautiful smile and musical voice, and the fervent soul breathing through both.

But to my story. Mrs. Brotherton, to complete her portrait, generally wore a black satin dress, with a fine white muslin handkerchief folded over her bosom, and a plain cap of lace on her head. Mrs. Brotherton's character was very remarkable for three qualities — high family pride, warm benevolence of heart, and great romance of mind. Her benevolence always kept her pride in check, so that it never became arrogant, but was only manifested in her great solicitude in keeping her children from forming acquaintances or connexions with the *nouveaux riches* of the neighborhood. Her benevolence had made great inroads upon her small fortune, and, for her thirdly-mentioned distinguishing trait, her romance of disposition, so far swept her flights of fancy, that, at the age of sixty, she would look upon her beautiful Sybil, and wish she could send her "home," as she fondly termed Old England, where she felt sure her lovely child would captivate some baron, earl, or duke. There was one rare feature in her mind more charming than even her benevolence. It was the simple, child-like trustfulness of disposition, that led her to reverse the rule of the worldling, and to believe every man and woman to be perfectly good, until she had experimentally found them to be otherwise.

Sybil Brotherton was a slight, fair girl, with a broad white forehead, large pensive blue eyes, and a sweet smile; a child of gentle and graceful movements, of low sweet tones, and of loving and pious heart. Sybil, too, was fanciful — she could not have been otherwise — and so, gently as she treated her partners at the village dancing-school, she thought them all sadly unlike the courtly Sir Charles Grandison and the stately Lord Mortimer; and she set down this world of reality to be a marvelously "flat, stale, and unprofitable" place to live in, and life itself, without a handsome and rich lover, to be a very dull story founded upon fact.

CHAPTER II.

THE MESSENGER — THE NOVEL READERS.

IT was evening, the ground was covered with snow, and the last rays of the setting sun lit up into blazing splendor the icicles pendant from the pine trees that crowned the hills surrounding Brotherton Hall. In a quaint old wainscoted parlor, before a blazing hickory fire, sat Mrs. Brotherton and Sybil. The old lady was employed in knotting a valance, the young one in tambouring a muslin apron. Before them stood a little, round, spider-legged tea-table, covered with a damask cloth, and set out with a service of grotesque old china.

"It is growing dusky, my dear child; ring for Broom to bring in the lights," said Mrs. Brotherton, as she rolled up her valance, and put it in her basket.

Sybil complied by putting away her own work and ringing a little silver hand-bell that stood upon the table. There were no bell wires running through the house, like nerves through a human body, in those days, reader.

The door opened, and, in answer to the summons, an old gray-haired servant appeared, with a candle in each hand. "Making a reverence" as he entered, he set the light upon the table, saying, as he did so —

"Madam, a man from Colonel John Henry Hines is waiting without. He brings a message for you."

"Bring him in, Broom."

"Yes, madam," and, with a second obeisance, the old man left the room.

There was this peculiarity about Mrs. Brotherton and her household, that, from a limited intercourse with the world, and a familiar acquaintance with stately old dramas and novels of the last century, the old lady had acquired a somewhat stiff and courtly manner of speaking and acting, except when thrown off her guard by strong feeling. This stately manner was particularly admired by her two old servants, Katy and Broom, both of whom copied it upon all possible occasions.

"Sarvint, madam — sarvint, miss," bowed the smart footman of Colonel Hines, as he entered the presence of the ladies.

"I understand you bear a message from Colonel Hines," said Mrs. Brotherton.

"Yes, madam; Colonel John Henry sends his 'spects, and says, with your permission, he will do himself the honor of calling, with his sister, in his carriage, to take Miss Brotherton to the ball to-morrow evening."

"Convey my grateful acknowledgments to Colonel Hines, and inform him that I shall be pleased to consign Miss Brotherton to his guardianship for the evening."

Overawed by the dignity and bewildered by the

eloquence of the old lady, the man bowed and left the room, followed by Broom.

"Broom!" said he, "what the old 'oman mean by that? She going to let the gal go?"

"Mr. Trimble!" said Broom, drawing himself up stiffly, "in de first place, *my* name is Mr. Broomley, and not Broom; *my lady* is Madam Brotherton, and no old woman; and my *young* lady is Miss Brotherton of Brotherton Hall, and no gal."

"Well, then, but what am I to tell the Colonel? That she is going to let the gal — I mean the young lady — go?"

"Bress your stupidity, Mrs. Brotherton is pleased to 'sign Miss Brotherton to his garden for the evening."

"'Fore de Lord, I don't know what that is; but I shall tell Colonel Hines that she is going to let the gal go."

"Look here, you man in livery, you green and yellow poll parrot, if you call Miss Brotherton a gal again, I'll cane you; so be off with the message, now," said old Broom, flourishing his blackthorn stick.

The man went his way, and old Broom went again into the kitchen to carry in tea. Having set supper upon the table, and seen the ladies seated, he took his stand behind the chair of Mrs. Brotherton.

"There, you may leave the room now, Broom. If we should need anything, Miss Brotherton will ring."

The old man went out.

"Now, my dear Sybil," said the old lady, "but for the kind attention of Colonel Hines, I should not permit you to attend this ball, for I do not wish the face of my granddaughter to be seen too often at these village balls."

"Indeed, dear grandmother, if Colonel Hines is to attend me there, I would rather not go."

"And *why*, my dear? What objections have you to Colonel Hines? Is he not very polite and attentive?"

"Yes, madam, oppressively so."

"Then, permit me to inform you that the attentions of Colonel Hines are a distinguished honor, even to Miss Brotherton."

"Yet, indeed, dear grandmother, I would fain dispense with the honor."

"Explain your antipathy, if you please, Sybil."

"Why, in the first place, dear grandmother, he is quite an old gentleman, near forty, is he not?"

"Colonel Hines is forty-seven years of age, quite in the noon of life."

"And I, in the morning twilight," said Sybil, sadly.

"Any other objection, Sybil?"

"Then he is short and thick, and has a broad red face, and a bald head, and a big — that is, a large — I mean a stout — in a word, he is a round old gentleman, who gets into a great heat when he dances —"

"Miss Brotherton, I am shocked, I am humiliated, at your language," said the old lady, trying to look severely at her pet. "Now, do me the favor to ring for Broom to remove the tea-equipage."

When the table was cleared and the fire replenished —

"Now, Broom," said Mrs. Brotherton, "bring in the box of books that last arrived from Baltimore, and open it." The box was brought in, and the lid forced off, and the wealth of entertainment displayed, all in handsome bindings.

Old Broom was on his knees at the box, officiating as gentleman usher to the books.

"There, Broom, hand me that book in red — ah! 'Linda; or The Young Pilot of the Belle Creole.'"

"Oh! grandmother, let us read that — that must be very interesting."

"Here, my child, take it," said the old lady, forgetting her displeasure. "Hand me those others, Broom — 'The Planter's Northern Bride,' ah ha!" "Oh! grandmother, that! that! let's read *that* to-night." "Stay, my love, let us look further. You are too excitable," said the old lady, continuing her examination with intense interest. "'The Curse of Clifton,' 'The Deserted Wife,' 'The Lost Heiress'"—

"Indeed! oh, grandmother, that! that! we've heard so much about that—*do* let's read that to-night."

"Very well, then, my dear, lay it by. Here, Broom, take these books up stairs, and put them in the book-case; and then go and tell Katy to bring in half a dozen eggs and a bottle of port, (we will have some mulled wine before we retire to rest, darling," said she in a low voice to Sybil), "and then, Broom, if you and Katy wish, you can come in and listen to the reading." Much pleased, the old man hastened to execute his mission. Now, do not think, gentle reader, that there was any inconsistency between Mrs. Brotherton's pride and her practice of admitting her old domestics to her evening readings! Her people, as she called them, had grown up with her — they were old and tried servants, perfectly faithful and respectful. And she had long observed with what greedy ears they would linger in the room and listen while she read.

Well! old Katy soon brought in her knitting, and old Broom followed her with his cards and wool, and one sat on a low seat in one corner of the fire-place, and the other on a cricket in the opposite corner, quiet, attentive, and pleased. Mrs. Brotherton and Sybil sat before the fire, with a work-stand between them, upon which stood a brightly burning lamp, work-basket, scissors, snuffers, etc. The old lady wiped her spectacles, put them on, opened her book, and commenced reading, amid profound silence, to most attentive and interested auditors. Sybil employed herself with her tambour frame. When Mrs. Brotherton grew weary of reading aloud, she would pass the book to Sybil, and take up her knotting. Miss Brotherton would then lay aside her work and read for an hour; and in that way they would agreeably relieve each other until it was time to retire to rest. Then old Broom would mull the wine, lay the cloth, and set out a few light sponge cakes. After Mrs. Brotherton and Sybil had partaken of the refreshments, the remainder was carried into the kitchen, for the solace of the old servants. Family prayer concluded the evening, and the little circle separated for the night.

CHAPTER III.

THE BALL AND THE BEAUX.

THE next day was a busy one with Mrs. Brotherton and Sybil. At length, at seven o'clock, Miss Brotherton was arrayed for the festival. As I have never minutely described Sybil Brotherton, I had better do it now, while she is in her "best bib and tucker," when Katy declared she "looked like any angel" (angels don't wear white satin, mechlin lace, and pearls, Katy). Sybil Brotherton was rather below the middle stature, with a slender frame, yet full formed, with rounded and tapering limbs, and a grace so natural that every movement expressed the poetry of motion. Her forehead was broad, high, and white; her eyes large, clear, and blue; her lips full, glowing, and beautiful. Her complexion was of that delicate and transparent white, so seldom seen except in consumptives, and in her cheeks was burning that fire of death that so resembles the rich rose of health. Her dark brown hair fell in long and shining ringlets upon her graceful neck and rounded bosom. Her pure and delicate beauty was set off to advantage by the rich dress of white satin and mechlin lace, and the bandeau of pearls contrasted well with her dark hair. The carriage of Colonel Hines drew up before the door at eight o'clock, and Sybil, carefully wrapped in her velvet mantle and hood, was handed in, and driven off. On the morning after the ball, Mrs. Brotherton and Sybil were seated at breakfast, when the former said—

"You must now tell me, darling, whom you saw at the ball, and who were your partners in the dance."

"Well, dear grandmother, there was the same old set. The Etheringtons, and the Somervilles, and the Kinlocks, and the —— Oh! by the way,

Hector Kinlock presented the Hon. Meredith Mills, one of our Representatives in Congress. He is from the lower part of the county, but he has purchased Blocksley Place, and is coming to reside in this neighborhood."

"Ah! Meredith Mills. What sort of a person is he, my dear?"

"Why, he is a young man, talented, I rather think — agreeable — and — not married, grandma, if you mean that," said Sybil, with a sly smile.

"I am sorry to see you rather disposed to levity, my dear Sybil; pray avoid it. Meredith Mills — the name is familiar. Oh! yes; certainly, I know the family; a very old family, originally from Lincolnshire; came over with the Calverts; certainly, the Mills's of Meredith Place; and coming to live in our neighborhood; and not married" ——

"And very much smitten with Sybil Brotherton, and coming to see her this morning."

"Sybil!" exclaimed the old lady, gravely looking over the top of her spectacles.

"My dear grandmother, you know one must be merry the day after a ball, if they are not fatigued."

"And is Mr. Mills coming here this morning?"

"He said he would do himself the honor of calling on us this morning."

"And what did you reply?"

"Why, that Mrs. Brotherton would be happy to receive him."

"That was correct. Did you form any other new acquaintances, Sybil?"

"N—n—o, madam, none except"—

"Except whom?"

"Nobody, in fact, but"—

"But whom?"

"But a young gentleman who came with Mr. Mills."

"And who was he?"

"A young artist."

"Humph! you are reserved, Sybil. What was his name?"

"Middleton."

"And he was very agreeable."

"Dear grandmother, I never said so."

"And you were very much pleased with him."

"Dear grandmother! pleased with a gentleman at the first interview! I thought you had a better opinion of me."

The old lady smiled.

"Oh! a gentleman, was he? I thought you said he was a painter."

"An artist, grandmother, an artist; and surely an artist is a gentleman, if any man is."

"Humph! that depends on whether he paints for money or amusement. But I shall not in future trust you to the care of any one. When I cannot attend you myself to public places, you must remain at home."

They were interrupted by a knock at the hall door and the entrance of old Broom, who informed the ladies that two gentlemen, Mr. Mills and Mr. Middleton, had called and were waiting in the drawing-room.

"Go in and see them, my dear Sybil. I will come presently," said Mrs. Brotherton.

As Sybil entered the drawing-room, Mr. Middleton advanced and led her to a seat, with the courtly grace of "sixty years since," hoping that Miss Brotherton had suffered no inconvenience from the fatigue of the preceding evening, or from the ride through the night air.

Miss Brotherton had suffered no inconvenience, and was much obliged.

Sybil then addressed herself to Mr. Mills, and trusted that he would find the neighborhood pleasant and the neighbors agreeable.

Mr. Mills was pleased with the neighborhood, and anticipated much pleasure from a more intimate acquaintance with its residents.

At this moment the door opened, and Mrs. Brotherton entered. Both gentlemen arose from their seats, and Sybil named Mr. Mills — Mr. Middleton — Mrs. Brotherton. The latter gentleman met Mrs. Brotherton, led her to the sofa, and took a seat near her. Mrs. Brotherton expressed to Mr. Middleton her gratification at forming his acquaintance. Mr. Middleton bowed reverently, and expressed his deep sense of the honor conferred upon him. The conversation then became general. Mr. Middleton quite won the heart of Mrs. Brotherton, by descanting upon the beauties of Brotherton Hall, its antique look, its picturesque situation, its pleasant locality, etc. Mrs. Brotherton, in acknowledgment, begged that he would frequently honor the Hall with his presence. All this time, Miss Brotherton was trying to amuse the Hon. Meredith Mills, and was in no small degree astonished and pleased at the wondrous *penchant* her grandmother had conceived for "the portrait painter." The problem was soon solved. The gentlemen arose to take leave. Madam Brotherton hoped they would soon repeat their visit. The gentlemen declared that they should feel so happy in accepting her invitation, and they bowed themselves out. When the sound of their horses' feet had died away —

"Well! what do you think of our visitors, grandma?" asked Sybil, gayly.

"Why, my dear Sybil, I think Mr. Meredith Mills a remarkably handsome, intellectual, and polished young gentleman. Of Mr. Middleton, I had not much opportunity of judging. He, as I regretted to see, had his attention entirely engrossed by yourself during the whole time of his visit. One thing, however, did strike me. I never saw a fairer illustration of the fact that good blood will show itself through all disguises. Now, observe — those two men — they were both equally well dressed, perhaps equally well educated, and received in the same society; but now observe the difference. In Mr. Meredith Mills, you saw the high-bred air of a gentleman of family; in Mr. Middleton was equally visible the *mauvaise honte* of a low person. Mr. Mills was easy, graceful, and conversable; Mr. Middleton shy, awkward, and embarrassed. I never saw a fairer illustration of high-bred aristocracy and of upstart vulgarity."

Sybil listened to this disquisition, with eyes and lips wide open with astonishment.

"Why, my dear grandmother!" said she, "are you not under a mistake? Which of the gentlemen did you suppose to be Mr. Mills?"

"Why, of course, the Hon. Meredith Mills was the gentleman who conversed with *me*, while you were so much occupied with the other young person."

A smile flashed into the eyes and curled around the lips of Sybil for an instant, and vanished, as she said, seriously —

"My dear grandmother, it's all owing to my awkward presentation, I suppose; but you have made the most amusing mistake. The tall, handsome, graceful, accomplished, and high-bred man, who led you to the sofa, and who charmed you so much by his intellectual conversation, and whom you have so highly approved and praised, was Harold Middleton, the portrait painter; and the little drab-colored gentleman, in light hair and a gray coat, was the Hon. Meredith Mills, of Meredith Place."

"I hope you do not jest with me, Miss Brotherton," said the old lady, looking curiously, between surprise, pique, and embarrassment.

"Or rather, you hope I *do* jest, dear grandmother, but I speak truth; however, your rule, I suppose, still holds good. This is but an exception."

The old lady seemed consoled, and remarked, with a smile —

"There is one thing, however, that pleases me, my dear Sybil. It is, that you kept that young man, Middleton, at a proper distance, while you showed fitting respect for Mr. Meredith Mills."

Sybil smiled, but there was something sad, almost remorseful, in her smile.

CHAPTER IV.

"MY GRANDFATHER, LORD MAINWARING."

A FEW weeks passed away. Sybil met young Middleton often in society. Indeed, he even came often to the house, where Mrs. Brotherton, in consideration of the pressing invitation extended to him on his first visit, continued to treat him with civility, if, indeed, the charming manners of the young man had not put it out of her power to treat him otherwise. Then, his unembarrassed manner to Miss Brotherton led off the suspicion that his affections were interested in her. The following circumstance opened the eyes of Mrs. Brotherton to the real position of the parties.

Colonel Hines had proposed for the hand of Miss Brotherton; Mrs. Brotherton had made known his wishes to her granddaughter, who received the news of the revival and pressing of the obnoxious suit with so much agitation and distress, that Mrs. Brotherton perceived that her heart was no longer free, and, by her questions, soon ascertained who had become its master. Upon the same evening, it happened that young Middleton called, and was received by Mrs. Brotherton alone and coldly. Sybil was weeping in her own room. Young Middleton, perceiving the change in her manner, suspected the truth, for he had become well acquainted with the old lady's foible; he therefore soon arose to take his leave, remarking, as he did so,

"This is probably the last opportunity I shall have of paying my devoirs to the ladies of Brotherton Hall; for my grandfather, the Earl of Mainwaring, has written to command my immediate return to England."

"Sir! did I hear aright? Your grandfather, the Earl of Mainwaring!" exclaimed the old lady, thrown off her guard.

"Yes, madam," said young Middleton, quietly. "Permit me to wish you a good evening. Pray present my most respectful regards to Miss Brotherton. Good evening, madam."

"No, no; do not go yet. You must take leave of Sybil — and — pray do me the favor to touch the bell. Perhaps you would take some refreshments."

The young man complied with her request, and —

"Broom!" said she to the old servant who answered the summons, "go and give my compliments to Miss Brotherton, and ask her *why* she keeps us waiting thus, and desire her to come down; and, Broom, serve refreshments. Mr. Middleton has ridden far, and would like something. Mr. Middleton, *do* be seated."

A sinister smile flitted across the young man's countenance as he sat down. Greatly wondering at the summons, Sybil entered the room, followed by Broom with refreshments. The young man's hurry seemed now to have evaporated, as, eventually, did the strong necessity for his going to England. It was late when he left the house. Sybil pleaded fatigue, and retired soon to bed. Many a fine aërial castle did Mrs. Brotherton build that evening for her pet.

"Humph! indeed!" soliloquized the old lady, as she walked restlessly about her chamber floor. "Who would have thought it? Lord Mainwaring! I wonder whether young Middleton's father is the eldest son of the Earl, the heir to his titles and estates. I should like so much to know. Dear me! the Earl of Mainwaring! The Earl and *Countess* of Mainwaring! Lord and Lady Mainwaring! I will go to England with them — my *granddaughter*, Lady Mainwaring!" said the old lady, ringing all the changes on the coveted title. "I must have a wedding. I will get the best confectioner, and the best French cook to provide the breakfast. Then we must speak to Madame Modiste about furnishing the bridal dress and veil, and we must consult her upon the trousseau generally"—and "Countess of Mainwaring!" muttered the old lady, as she sank to sleep that night. "How well a coronet will grace that angel brow!"

"God help old madam!" said Katy to Broom that night at the kitchen fire, "she has been talking to herself all the evening."

Young Middleton's return to England was indefinitely postponed, and, before the trees had put forth their leaves, or the snow was melted off the ground, Sybil Brotherton was the wife of Harold Middleton. The young couple, much to the comfort of Mrs. Brotherton, had concluded to spend the first year of their married life at Brotherton Hall. Mrs. Brotherton had ascertained that the father of her son-in-law was the *third* son of Lord Mainwaring, and that at least three persons stood between him and the Earl's coronet. But at least he was the grandson of a peer, and that was much.

CHAPTER V.

THE YOUNG WIFE.

HOW soon was the sweet dream of Sybil broken! How soon the beautiful illusion of Sybil dispelled! How soon "the veiled prophet" of her idolatry stood forth in all his hideous deformity! A few months after their marriage, Harold Middleton began to absent himself from his young wife all day, and sometimes all night. The playful and loving expostulations of Sybil were kindly taken at first, and explanations, which she received with confiding affection, were given of his absence. But even this disguise was at last thrown off.

About twelve months after her marriage, Sybil was sitting reading with her grandmother, in their little parlor. Earlier than usual, the old lady complained of fatigue and drowsiness, and retired to rest. Sybil did not seek her chamber, but, desiring Broom to bring some refreshments, and sending Katy to her chamber for his dressing-gown and slippers, she drew her chair to the fire, to await the coming of her husband. She could not read, she laid her book down, her very face breathed joy. Sybil had ascertained that she would become a mother, and, with the confiding love of a young wife, she wished to make her husband a sharer of her joy. Long did Sybil wait, but not impatiently, for her face was still beaming with gentle happiness, when the sound of a horse's feet, followed by an impatient rap at the door, caused her to start joyfully up, and go to open it herself, exclaiming, as she met her husband —

"Oh! dear Harold, how glad I am that you have come at last! I have been waiting so long for you!"

Repulsing her offered caress, he said, sternly and angrily —

"I have before this intimated my desire that you should retire to rest at your usual hour, instead of sitting up for me, Mrs. Middleton. Do not give me occasion to repeat the injunction."

A woman of more spirit would have resented this; a woman of less sensibility might not have felt it. Poor Sybil, from the very manner of her education, as well as from her native temperament, was the victim of a morbid sensibility. This was the first occasion upon which Middleton had spoken unkindly to her, and she felt it deeply. Pale and trembling, she sank into her seat; Middleton threw himself upon the sofa. The coffee grew cold, the oysters became turbid in their liquor, the candles burned low, the fire died out, and Sybil's sweet news remained untold. Silent tears were stealing down her cheeks. This seemed rather to harden the heart of her husband, who now said, sternly —

"This course of conduct looks very like a wilful disregard of my wishes, Mrs. Middleton.

Perhaps they were not explained with sufficient clearness?"

Sybil started as the first angry tones of his voice fell upon her ears, then looking into his face with an expression of distressing inquiry, and meeting nothing there but sullen anger, she arose from her seat, and, taking her night-lamp, was about to leave the room. Seeming to take a second thought when she reached the door, she turned back, and, setting down her lamp, approached her husband, and putting her arms around his neck and pressing her lips upon his brow, she murmured —

"Do not be angry with me, dear Harold. I will not stay up for you another time, if you will love me now."

This caress was received in sullen silence, and not returned. The gentle words of Sybil remained unnoticed. Unclasping her arms, after a few moments, she withdrew to her chamber, and sought her pillow, where, like a child as she was, she soon wept herself to sleep.

"A poor, pale, whining creature," muttered Middleton, looking after his wife as she left the room. "If I had known that this old place was in chancery, I would have seen her in Jericho before I would have married her. Strange! that I never happened to hear it until to-night. And you, Inez! my bright, my beautiful, my dark-browed girl of Italy! Was it for this, I cast you away? No matter; fetters not riveted with gold fall easily from my wrists, bright Inez! And if this property should slip from its present possessors" —

Middleton fell into a deep revery, so that it was near morning when he retired to his chamber.

A few months passed, and the case in chancery was decided against the Brothertons, and a suit entered to eject them from the premises. From this time, the mask of hypocrisy assumed by Middleton, and which had occasionally slipped

aside, was now laid by for ever. With what
funds he could wrest from his gentle wife, or,
through her, from Mrs. Brotherton, he would frequent the county seat, and spend whole days and
nights in dissipation. Sybil grew pale and melancholy, and, having lost all esteem and respect
for her husband, took no further comfort in her
love; and, indeed, with her delicate health and
timid temper, she generally felt rather relieved,
when, after she had given him all the money she
could raise, he would take himself off for a week,
for then she felt secure, at least, from personal
violence and danger to herself and her unborn
babe; for, alas! Sybil Middleton, the delicate,
the sensitive, and the refined, had felt the weight
of her husband's hand in anger, had trembled for
her life in his presence. But these scenes of
violence would generally occur after Middleton
had been drinking freely. And Sybil had another
sorrow; she perceived, with grief and dismay,
that her beloved grandmother was falling into

premature dotage. The trials of the old lady's age had been too great for her to bear. The loss of the Brotherton estate, the unworthiness of her son-in-law, the misery of her darling granddaughter, and the prospective ejectment from the home of her youth, all pressed upon the old lady's mind, and at length broke it down.

CHAPTER VI.

THE YOUNG MOTHER.

"STAY with me to-night, dear Harold; I am ill, and I am frightened. Stay with me to-night," pleaded Sybil, timidly taking the hand of her husband as he was about to leave the house.

"I am not a physician, Mrs. Middleton," replied he, coldly.

"Yet you are more to me — the only one who can give me comfort and strength in my coming trial. I am weak and fearful. I know I am a fool, yet bear with me a while, and — stay with me to-night."

"You have your grandmother with you."

"Alas! my poor grandmother! she herself needs care and attention. She is incapable of giving me comfort. Oh! do not leave me!"

exclaimed she suddenly, catching his hand, as he was about to go. "Stay with me to-night."

"You are importunate, Mrs. Middleton," said he, releasing himself, "and I regret to say that I cannot comply with your request. Good-evening." And he left the room.

Sybil turned aside to weep, but wiped her tears hastily away, as she perceived her poor grandmother totter into the room.

"Weeping again, Sybil, my poor child?" said the old lady, sinking into a chair, and holding out her arms to her granddaughter. "Come to my bosom, my dear child. What is your grief, Sybil?"

"Nothing, my dear grandmother, only I am not very well," said Mrs. Middleton, pleased, yet wondering at the temporary revival of the old lady's intellect.

"No, my poor child; you are far from well. I see that. You must go to bed, Sybil, and I will send for a physician. Katy! tell Broom to saddle a horse, and ride over to Doctor Hall's, and ask him to come over directly; that Mrs. Middleton is ill; and, Katy, do you carry an armful of wood up into your young lady's chamber. Lean on me, my dear Sybil, and come up stairs."

Lean on her! Poor old trembler! There was something inexpressibly touching in her protection of Sybil, while she herself so much needed support.

Mrs. Middleton gained her room, and was assisted to bed. Mrs. Brotherton took her seat in a large arm-chair by her side. Sybil repressed her complaints, that she might not give pain to the tender-hearted old lady. The physician lived ten miles off; the night was far advanced, and he had not yet arrived. Sybil lay perfectly quiet and silent, except when she would entreat her grandmother to go to rest, and leave old Katy to watch.

"No, no, darling; no, no, my poor child," would be the old lady's answer.

Sybil at last said —

"Dear grandmother, I would like to go to sleep, but I cannot sleep while I see you there. Will you not retire to bed?"

"Are you better, then, my love? I am so glad! Well, as soon as I see you asleep, I will go!"

"Good-night, then, dear grandmother!"

"God bless you, darling!"

Sybil closed her eyes and affected to sleep. After a few moments, the old lady arose and looked over her, but she could not see by the dim light of the taper the corrugated brow and the clenched hands of the sufferer.

"She is asleep!" murmured the old lady. "Bless her, poor thing, I was afraid she was going to be sick." And she glided from the room, telling Katy that she would dispense with her services for that night, and charging her to sleep by the bedside of her young lady, in case she should need any thing.

In an hour after, Sybil Middleton pressed her first-born child to her bosom.

"Thank God for my beautiful boy! Thank God for my spared life!" fervently exclaimed the exhausted mother, as she received the babe in her arms.

"Now, my dear young lady, as you are comfortable, hadn't I better wake madam?"

"No, Katy; let her sleep, and I must rest now. How proud Harold will be of his son! How happy poor grandmother will feel that my trial is safely over!" was the last thought of Sybil, as she sank to rest.

"Oh! my dear young lady! my dear young lady!" exclaimed old Katy, bursting into the chamber of Mrs. Middleton at early dawn.

"Why, what is the matter, Katy?" inquired Sybil, in affright.

"Your poor grandmother! your good old grandmother!"

"Katy! what *is* the matter? What of my dear grandmother?"

"Dead in her bed! dead in her bed!"

With a smothered shriek, Sybil fell back on her pillow.

Old Broom, who, unable to find the Doctor, had returned late at night, was despatched to Colonel Hines's. The Colonel and his sister quickly obeyed the summons, and hastened to Brotherton Hall. The family physician also arrived early in the morning, and a messenger was despatched to Mr. Middleton. In the mean time, Colonel Hines and his sister Rachel took the direction of affairs; and truly the kind offices of these good Samaritans were needed, for Mrs. Brotherton had expired during the night in a fit of apoplexy, and Mrs. Middleton was lying extremely ill and delirious. Mr. Middleton returned late in the evening. On the fourth day from her decease, the funeral of Mrs. Brotherton took place. It was attended by all the gentry of the neighborhood. The wild delirium of Mrs. Middleton had been subdued, but she lay in a stupor, insensible to all that was passing around her. Miss Rachel Hines kindly volunteered to remain at Brotherton Hall to nurse the invalid.

At length Sybil was raised from her bed of illness, and, in a fortnight from the day on which she first sat up, she left her room. Miss Rachel Hines had returned home. It was evening, and Sybil said to herself —

"I will surprise Harold, and please him, by joining him at tea."

And wrapping her shawl around her, she descended to the parlor. Old Broom was just setting tea upon the table as she entered. In answer to her inquiry, the old man told her that Mr. Middleton was talking with a strange man in the entry. Desiring Katy to go up and remain with her infant, and telling Broom to be in waiting upon the table, Sybil took her seat. Middleton entered, and as he sat down in his place, remarked —

"I am glad to see you out of your chamber,

Sybil, for we shall be obliged to get out of the house very soon."

"As you please, dear Harold. I am ready to accompany you, when and where you please."

Harold Middleton smiled darkly.

"But it is not as I please, Mrs. Middleton. Let me tell you, it is far more easy to get rid of one handsome establishment than to find another."

Not comprehending the cause of his ill-humor, but seeing from his inflamed face that he had been drinking, Sybil answered gently and soothingly——

"Dearest Harold, believe me, I am willing to do just as you see fit. I had as lief remain here as go elsewhere, if you prefer it."

"You are dull, Mrs. Middleton; you do not seem to comprehend that a writ of ejectment has been served upon us, and that we *must* go."

"Oh! it is sad, indeed, to leave our home upon compulsion. But, dearest Harold, do not call me Mrs. Middleton, and speak so coldly to me. You know I have no one to love me now but you."

"You are irritable, and not very agreeable, this evening, Mrs. Middleton. I think you have left your chamber too soon; I advise you to return to it."

Sybil left the room.

On the morning succeeding this conversation, Middleton left home for Baltimore, and was absent about a week. At the end of that time he returned, and, entering the parlor, where his wife sat at work, informed her that he had received a letter from his father requiring his immediate presence in London to attend a lawsuit; and that he should go in the next ship, which would sail in two weeks.

"Very well, dear Harold, we must make some provision for the two poor old people in the kitchen, and I shall be so glad to go. I like the arrangement very much. I shall be delighted to cross the ocean, and so happy, so very happy, to know your father and mother. I shall find parents again in them; and they will be *so* pleased, will they not, to see our babe, their grandchild? Oh! yes; I shall be quite ready in a week."

"Well! have you done, Sybil?"

Sybil raised her large, tender eyes to his countenance with an inquiring glance, and remained silent.

"I never contemplated taking *you* to England, Sybil; at least when I go. I do not indeed know how you would be received by my family. It will take, I fear, some considerable diplomacy to reconcile my father to this somewhat inconsiderate marriage of mine."

The blood rushed to the face of Sybil, and the tears to her eyes; to conceal which, she stooped and raised her babe from the cradle.

"But this is my design. I will attend promptly my father's summons; meet him in

London, and, after the hurry of business is over, I will endeavor to reconcile him to our marriage, then send or come for you and the child."

Mrs. Middleton was reassured by his words, especially as his manner was kinder than usual, and he had called her "Sybil" through the conversation. She inquired —

"And how long will it be, dear Harold, before you send?"

"Oh! in a few months from this — in the fall, probably; and, in the mean time, I will take a house for you in Baltimore for the summer."

"It seems a long time until the fall; but then I suppose I am weak to feel so," said Sybil, repressing a sigh.

The next few days were employed in selling off the furniture and plate at Brotherton Hall. A few family portraits and some pieces of old-fashioned furniture were reserved for the use of Mrs. Middleton during the summer.

Two weeks from this time, Sybil found herself

the occupant of a small cottage in the suburbs of Baltimore. Katy was retained in her service, upon reduced wages; and old Broom, who had " saved a penny," went to live with some of his relations.

It was the morning of Middleton's departure. His trunks were all on board, and the ship he was going out in was to sail with the first tide.

At early dawn, Middleton and Sybil stood at the cottage gate.

"And will you *indeed* send for me in the fall, dear Harold?" said Sybil, sadly.

"Why, *certainly*, Sybil; why do you doubt me?" said Middleton, smilingly.

"I do not doubt you, but I love to hear you promise again and again."

"Well, I must be gone; farewell, Sybil."

"Good-by! good-by! — Oh! come back; let me take a long, long look into your eyes — a look that will last me till we meet" ——

"Well! will that do, Sybil? There — there

—I must go. Be cheerful; farewell. I will send for you soon."

And they parted; he with a lie on his lips, rejoicing in his release; she to her lonely hearth, profoundly grateful for his seeming kindness, and building many bright hopes upon his faithless promises.

CHAPTER VII.

KATY'S MISHAPS IN THE CITY.

THE leaves were falling, and the cold northwest wind was blowing them in drifts about the cottage of Mrs. Middleton. Old Katy was roaming about the garden, gathering sticks to make a fire; in the course of her gleaning, she passed into the front yard. Seeing the figure of an old man leaning on a stick at the gate, she dropped her bundle and hastened forward, joyfully exclaiming —

"Lor' a' mercy upon me, Broom! Is this *you?* *Is* this you? Bless your ole soul, I am *so* glad to see you once again in this worl'! Come in, come in; how have you been this long time?"

"Thanky, Katy, thanky; I'm so-so, 'cept the rheumatics, and the phthisic, and the asthma and lumbago, and the liver complaint, and the consumption, except that I enjoys pretty good health in general."

"'Deed! I'm glad to hear you're so hearty. It's more than I am; I'm troubled with a stiff neck."

"Yes! you were always stiff-necked, Katy."

Now, Broom, that was a libel on Katy!

"Well, Katy, how is the young madam and the little child, and when is she going to foreign parts?"

"Ah! poor dear child! I think she's in a 'sumption, Broom. She used to be purty as a picter, Broom; now she's all pale and thin, and her eyes are hollow. She's never hearn a word from that vilyun (God forgive me) that she married. She's gone to the pos' office now, poor dear heart, to see if there's a letter for her. She seen in a newspaper how the ship that *he* went out in has comed back, and so she's gone. But come in, Broom, out o' the cold; you shall see the child, poor little cretur, by the kitchen fire—

no! by the kitchen fire-place—no fire there! Dunno when there will be."

"Why, you don't go to make out how the young madam wants for anything, do ye?"

"Don't want for nothing, don't she? I tell you, Broom, that vilyun (mercy on me) never left her a single dollar—made out he'd want all the money to carry him to foreign parts. *I* know, 'cause, you see, she wanted tea and sugar the day after he went away; and so she sent her silver spoons to be sold—sent 'em by me; and by the same token, the silversmiff where I took them took the spoons away from me, and sent for a cons'able, and had me 'rested on 'spicion of stealing them; yes! and 'rested me there all day, till the young lady could be sent for. Lor', Broom, how my feelings were hurted that day! that ever Catherine Ann Gallagher should be 'rested for stealin' silver spoons! You don't know how I was hurt!"

"I can 'magine, Katy; I can 'magine. You

know, though, you used to hear the ole madam say, as none of the people in cities ever come ober with Lord Baltimore, so how can you 'spect better from them?"

"Well, I was going to tell you, Broom — but come in out of the wind — there's the baby! The very image of the old madam, aint he? There! don't wake him; sit down. I was a-going to tell you, that after that, the young madam always wrote a line when she sent me to sell anything; and she sold almost all the silver she had, to buy things and pay rent; for only think, Broom, people here have to pay for living in houses!"

"Pshaw! I could have told you that long ago."

"I didn't know it. Well, there's nothing left to sell, now, but the blade of the butter knife and her thimble — that's *silver*, I mean; and what we are to do, now the winter's setting in, the Lord knows. We been living on black tea and rye bread all this summer. The poor child wanted me to go hire out where I could get wages and better living; but no, I says; if I've got a black skin, I've got a white soul; and I aint agoing to 'sert her in her 'fliction."

"No, no more I wouldn't, Katy. Dear, dear, dear," sighed the old man; "this is *very* 'stressing, very! But couldn't the young lady teach the pianner, or paint picters, or diskiver some rich relations, like the 'stressed ladies in the story books, she used to read to us about?"

"Well, I often thinks o' that myself; and I thinks, what's the good o' larnin' unless it helps people to get along in the world. But, poor thing! her mind is 'sturbed enough. Sometimes she does walk about a whole day, looking for needlework; but she is a stranger, and gets no luck, and she comes home, and mopes, and mopes, I 'vises her to smoke a pipe; but she won't take 'vice. I tells her, if it hadn't a been for smoking a pipe, I should have gone ravin' 'stracted mad, when Colonel Hines (Heaven forgive him) sold my poor dear gal to Georgy. My poor gal! my poor gal! your poor old mother will never see you again in this world. My poor dear gal! all the child I had in the world!" Here the poor old soul lost recollection of everything but her own sorrow, and sobbed hysterically.

"Don't cry, Katy! don't cry! that's a good 'oman!"

"Hush, Broom, hush! you never had no child sold away from you."

"No, Katy, because my wife was sold away from me the first year we were married, and I never had the heart to marry again."

"My poor gal! my poor child!"

"Come, Katy, don't take on so; don't, that's a dove!"

When the old creature had exhausted herself with weeping, she wiped her eyes. Then Broom said to her —

"You never told me, Katy, how it was that you were free and your child a slave."

"Why, you see, Broom, I was left to Colonel Hines by his uncle, but I was left to be free at twenty-five; and I had my little gal before I had served my time out, and so she was a slave. I had been living with Mrs. Brotherton ever since I was ten years old, and I was there when my poor gal was sold. She tried to prevent it, but couldn't. You were gone with Colonel Brotherton to the wars then. Don't ask me any more, please, Broom;" and the old creature fell to weeping again. At last, wiping her eyes, she said—

"Well, well! well, well! may be it will all come right in another world. Give me that bundle of chips, Broom; I must make a cup of tea for Mrs. Middleton, against she comes. I wish I had a little wood, to make a fire in her room."

"Now, you stop, old 'oman. How long before she'll be back?"

"An hour or so."

"Well!" said the old man, brightening up, "I'll just tell you what I goin' to do. I goin' after a load of wood and a basket of good things; and I'll just have 'em brought home, and don't you let on who sent them, 'cause the young lady might feel bad at 'ceiving a favor from the likes o' me, 'cause that's a little worser than anything we ever heard about in the books at night."

The old man was as good as his word. In an hour a blazing fire was kindled in Sybil's room, and the tea-table spread with nice white bread and fresh butter, while a pot of fragrant hyson was drawing on the hearth. The babe was awake, sitting on the carpet, blowing a whistle with great glee. At last Sybil entered, pale, languid, and weary, and, dropping into a chair, held out her arms to the babe, who crawled fast upon his hands and knees to reach her lap.

"Ah! she's got no letter," thought old Katy, as she came in to set the tea on the table.

"The silversmiff has been here, ma'am (Heaven forgive me for lying,") muttered she to herself.

"The silversmith, Katy!"

"Yes, ma'am; and he fotch two dollars, as he said was due on the spoons; and so I took the money, ma'am, and bought some wood and some other things; (Heaven look over fibbing.")

"Very well, Katy, that was a Godsend, indeed; but you left the babe to do this."

"No, ma'am; old Uncle Broom 'rived this morning, and I got him to go."

"Poor old man! Has he traveled all the way up here? Send him in to see me, Katy."

"'Scuse me, Mrs. Middleton; but did you get a letter, ma'am?"

"No, Katy; but to-morrow I will go and see the captain of the ship he went out in; perhaps he has a letter or a message for me."

CHAPTER VIII.

THE CAPTAIN'S NEWS.

THE next morning, after an early breakfast, Sybil put her babe to sleep, and went her way in search of the captain of the ship in which her husband had left America. In going towards the ship, she had to pass through crowds of coarse women and rough men, whose ribaldry caused her nerves to tremble and her cheek to burn with shame. At length, finding it difficult to reach the ship, which was lying off the shore, she inquired where the captain was likely to be found, and was directed to his lodgings in the city. She hurried thither, was so lucky as to find him at home, and was shown into his presence. He was a fat, red-faced, self-satisfied looking man, who arose to receive her with rather an insolent leer.

"You are Captain Blackston, I presume?"

"At your service, miss."

"I am Mrs. Middleton."

"Ah! I beg your pardon, madam."

"My husband, Mr. Harold P. Middleton, went to Liverpool in your ship about four months since. I have come to inquire whether you have any letter or message from him for me, and whether he was in good health when he landed."

"Whew!" whistled the captain.

"Will you please to tell me, sir?"

"Why, madam, here seems to be a great mystery. Mr. Middleton, certainly, was my passenger to Liverpool; but he took with him a lady whom he called Mrs. Middleton, and whom I supposed to be his wife. Heavens! ma'am, don't faint here in my room!" exclaimed the captain, seizing the bell rope, and ringing an alarm.

"William!" cried he, energetically, to the man that answered the bell, "call a hackney coach for this lady."

Sybil mastered her emotion by a great effort, and entered the coach that had been called for her, for indeed her trembling limbs refused to convey her home. It took Sybil's last dollar, the produce of the sale of the butter-knife, to pay her fare. For many days, Sybil remained almost stupefied with grief, sometimes wandering restlessly about, sometimes sitting for hours in one mournful position, sometimes catching up her infant, and weeping passionately over it. Poor old Katy was distressed almost to death, but could not guess the cause of her acute sorrow. A few weeks from this time Sybil saw a letter advertised for her in the paper. Too weak to go herself, she hurried old Katy off to the post-office. Poor old Katy was always sure to fall into adventures, when she was sent into the city. When she arrived at the post-office, and was asked by the clerk what she wanted, she answered—

"That letter, if you please, sir."

"What letter, aunty?"

"Why, the letter from foreign parts, if you please."

"Yes; but whose letter?"

"Why, hizzen, sir, hizzen."

"What name, old woman?"

"Why, Mr. Middleton, the gentleman as went to foreign parts."

The clerk looked over his list, and answered —

"There is nothing here for Mr. Middleton."

"The letter ain't for Mr. Middleton, sir."

"For whom then, old woman?" said the clerk, growing impatient.

"Miss Sybil that was, sir — Miss Sybil Brotherton, of Brotherton Hall, come over with Lord Baltimore, sir," said Katy, curtsying at every clause.

"There is no letter here for Miss Brotherton."

"She's not Miss Brotherton now; she's Mrs. Middleton."

"Why, what a stupid old beast is this! Here, here is your letter."

"Thanky, sir! very kind of you, indeed, sir; thanky, kindly. I wouldn't take a golden guinea for this letter."

It was raining hard when Katy left the office, and she looked around in despair — for Katy had no umbrella. A hackney coach was standing near, and Katy looked longingly at it. Observing this, the driver said, jeeringly —

"A hack, ma'am?"

"Thank you, kindly; yes, sir, if you please."

Finding a customer, the driver changed his tone, opened the door, and handed the old woman in with respectful alacrity, and closing the door again, jumped into his seat, and drove off.

"Dear me!" said old Katy, as she sat back in the carriage. "This is very nice and comfortable — so much better than sploshing through the mud and getting wet to the skin. I love the motion of a carriage, too — it tintillates one's feelings so pleasantly. What a very polite young man, to offer me a ride — so different from other people. Ain't he got manners? I shouldn't wonder if his family didn't come over with Lord Baltimore. What nice soft cushions!"

The end of this soliloquy brought Katy to Mrs. Middleton's door. The "very polite young man" jumped from his seat, and, opening the door, handed Katy out.

"I am very much obliged to you, indeed, sir, for your kindness, sir. I'll do you a favor whenever I have a chance."

"Very well; you're quite welcome; your money is just as good as anybody's else. It's a dollar."

"Sir?"

"It's a dollar."

"What's a dollar?"

"It's a dollar you owe me for bringing you home in my hack."

"Why, you invited me to ride in your hack, I never asked you; it was your own offer, and I thank you kindly. But you're not going to charge me, now, I hopes."

"Come, that's rich."

"Good-morning; I thank you kindly; I must go in now."

"Look here, old woman; none of your nonsense; hand me that dollar."

"I shan't do no such a thing! I shan't do no such a thing! You 'vited me to take a ride, and I rid; and now I know it was all to cheat me out of a dollar."

"See here, you old devil, if you don't pay me that dollar, I'll put you in the hands of a constable for swindling."

"Now, the mercy upon me; where am I to get a dollar from?"

Words now grew so high between the belligerent parties, that the noise drew Mrs. Middleton to the door; and great was her perplexity when she understood the cause of dispute — for poor Sybil was penniless. Telling Katy that she was in the wrong, and explaining to the hackman Katy's mistake, and promising to pay him the next day, Sybil separated the combatants, and, receiving her letter, she retired to read it. She opened it eagerly. There was no enclosure; and merely remarking that little Hubert would go without his flannel some time longer, she began to read. Her cheek grew pale and paler as she read, the letter dropped from her hand, and she sat as one stricken with epilepsy. Presently, the blood rushed back in torrents to her face, and, clasping her hands to her throbbing temples, she started up and paced the floor with irregular steps, exclaiming —

"Oh! the fiend! the fiend! — yet not the fiend, either, for there is something large about the devil, after all — the reptile! the reptile, rather! Coldly to tell me he does not care for me — falsely to tell me that he suspects my fidelity — to renounce his wife, to disown his child, and slander both, to color his baseness!

Where sleeps the justice of God? What stays the thunderbolt, that it does not strike him down in his rampant wickedness?" And Sybil threw herself, writhing, upon the bed. The scathing thunder and lightning of passion passed, and the rain fell. Sybil wept as she murmured —

"Oh, Harold! Harold! I never thought to have felt towards thee thus! I never thought to have spoken of you so!"

Sybil sat, pale, exhausted, and alarmed, at the typhoon that had passed through her gentle soul.

"Great God!" said she, "this, then, is passion! this, then, is anger! Oh! now, indeed, I know there is no need of a lake of burning fire; our bosoms may be a hell, as mine has just proved; our own passions may be tormenting fiends, if there be no others."

Sybil sunk upon her knees and prayed; and from this moment may be dated the commencement of her true knowledge of God, of herself, of the value of life and the use of suffering, of the reality of another and a happier state of existence. Amid the confusion, the storm, the whirlwind of her excited passion, arose "the still small voice" that whispered, "Peace, be still," and "Be not afraid; it is I." Sybil arose from her prayer, calm, composed; prospects became clearer before her mental vision, and she thought —

"Though it is all over now with me and my husband, yet, now that I know the worst, I can bear it! I have no further thoughts of going to him. I must bestir myself to find some means of support for myself and child. I will trust to God's blessing on my best exertions. I will work and pray; and I shall succeed, I know I shall."

With newly inspired courage, Sybil put on her bonnet and shawl, and went to the door; but the rain, that again came down in torrents, arrested her purpose of going out.

Sybil was a good performer on the piano and

harp, and she sought to obtain pupils in her art; but she was a stranger, without letters of introduction, and her efforts of course failed of success. She then thought of writing to her relative, General Bushrod Brotherton, the successful litigant in the suit in chancery, and the present possessor of Brotherton Hall. She wrote, and, telling him of her destitution, requested him to obtain for her the testimonials of some of her former neighbors.

CHAPTER IX.

GENERAL BUSHROD BROTHERTON.

A WEEK from this time she went to the post-office, hoping to receive her expected packet of testimonials. Before she came home a storm of wind and snow arose and raged with great violence. Old Katy stood at the cottage gate, looking the picture of dismay, and whispering to herself —

"Poor thing! she'll catch her death; and then all her troubles will be over!"

In the midst of Katy's lamentation, a traveling carriage drew up before the door, a servant jumped off from behind, let down the steps, and an old gentleman, with a military air, alighted and walked towards the house.

"Well! bress the Lord! if here ain't General

Bushrod Brotherton himself!" exclaimed Katy, in a low voice, as she hastened to open the gate.

"Well, old woman! *Katy*, are you not?"

"Yes, sir — Katy, sir — yes, sir," answered the old woman, curtsying at every two words.

"She's gone out, sir; she'll soon be home, sir. Will you come in?"

General Brotherton followed the old servant into the house, and in half an hour after, Sybil came home. Katy was on the watch for her, and, meeting her, said —

"Oh! Mrs. Middleton! who you think is here, ma'am? General Brotherton is in the house. Come round the kitchen way, to change your dress. I stole your best gown out of your room, for you to put on there."

Be it known to the reader, that there was no getting into Sybil's chamber but through the parlor; hence Katy's little piece of finesse. Sybil changed her dress quickly, and went into the parlor.

"My dear Mrs. Middleton, or my sweet cousin Sybil — if you will permit me to call you so — how pleased I am at this opportunity of making your acquaintance!" cordially exclaimed General Brotherton, advancing to meet her. General Brotherton was a tall, stout man, with a broad, rosy, good-humored face, and gray hair. Sybil was rather prepossessed with his appearance, and received him kindly and gracefully. After a little unimportant conversation, and a few remarks that led to the subject, General Brotherton observed —

"I hope, my dear little cousin Sybil, you will do me the justice to believe that I would never have molested Mrs. Brotherton in the possession of her home during her life."

"Had she lived," replied Sybil, "Mrs. Brotherton would have acknowledged the kind intention, as I do, with deep gratitude."

"There is more I wished to say to you, my dear cousin Sybil; but I am a blunt old man, and may not know how to approach the subject with the necessary tact and delicacy, perhaps; and I may offend when I desire to please. If I do, you will forgive me, will you not, my dear cousin? Well, this is what I wished to say: First, I have received your letter, and that has brought me to town. Of that, more anon. Well; at the time my attorney entered suit for possession of the Brotherton property, I had heard that Mrs. Brotherton was dead, and that you, Sybil, had been some time married to a wild young fellow, the son of a man of wealth and family, and that you were both soon going to England. Hence the suit. But within a month, my dear cousin Sybil, I have heard another story—that my cousin's husband was an impostor and a villain; that he has left her and her child in poverty and want, excusing his base desertion by charging her with conjugal infidelity."

Sybil covered her burning face with her hands.

"Oh, Lord!" she groaned, "I did not know, I did not dream, any one but myself knew of this!"

"It is all over our neighborhood; but, of course, no one believes the wicked lie."

"You need not tell me that, sir," exclaimed Sybil, suddenly assuming the air of an outraged empress. "It is not within the wide range of possibility that my bitterest enemy, even were he the most credulous of fools, *could* believe such a thing! And I only wonder that any one should allude in my presence to such a story."

"There, there," muttered the General, seemingly much mortified, "I knew I should offend — I am such a rough old wretch — I blurt things out so."

His manner touched Sybil, and produced a reaction in her feelings. She hastened to say —

"Forgive me, my dear sir; much trouble has made me very irritable, and I cannot bear the least allusion to that subject."

"Very well! All's right! Now, to come to the point and purpose of my visit. He has left you — that is plain. He has taken a foreign girl out with him — one Inez — Inez de — I forget! but I heard all about it. Well! I have no nearer relation than you in the world; and if you will return with me to Brotherton Hall, and live with me and my old wife, and be our daughter, and if you will apply to the Legislature for a divorce, and have your son's name changed to that of Brotherton, I will execute a will, leaving, at my death, all the Brotherton property to you for your lifetime, and afterwards to your son. Come, Sybil, what say you?"

The vision of wealth, comfort, ease, and her child's interest, arose before her "mind's eye," her heart beat quickly, her face flushed.

"Come, my dear little cousin! what say you?"

The "still small voice" whispered the moral bearing of the question, and Sybil's heart paused in its violent beatings to listen — the flush died away from her face.

"Come, my dear Sybil, your answer."

"Will you give me a few days to think of this,

my dear sir? and in the mean time believe me most grateful, most deeply grateful, for your kindness."

"Selfishness, pure selfishness, dear Sybil. My wife and I are lonesome in the old house; we want company. Think of my proposition a whole week, if you will — I don't like hasty decisions myself; but give me an answer at the end of that time. But mind, cousin Sybil, my conditions are positively unalterable — for I know very well, if *one* condition is not insisted upon, that just as soon as my old head is laid low, and you in possession of Brotherton Hall, that fellow would be sneaking back, and then you'd receive him. I know — oh! I know you women so well. He'd be so penitent! and you so forgiving! and in five or six years the Brotherton estate would be lost at the faro table, and you would be beggared. Oh! I know — I know so well!" So saying, the old man took leave, entered his carriage, and was driven off.

Now, this proposition would not have tempted Sybil, had a single spark of affection or esteem for her husband remained in her bosom; but it was not so. Her regard for Middleton had rather been a girlish fancy, than a woman's deep affection; though, with a woman of Sybil's domestic tastes and affectionate heart, this regard would have deepened into love, had not all respect been so soon lost. It was not his dissipation, nor his brutality, nor even his desertion of her, that had alienated the heart of his wife, but the cold, fierce, determined malignity of mind — the unmixed, unredeemed, unredeemable depravity of heart manifested throughout their entire married life, but most plainly discovered in the only letter he had ever written to her. Sybil's heart, therefore, was not defended against the solicitations of self-interest and maternal love by any affection lingering there. The test of principle could therefore be fairly applied to her unguarded, unsupported heart.

When the old man was gone, Sybil sat down to consider. She was a stranger and friendless; her money was all spent, and her plate and jewelry all sold; her store of fuel and provisions nearly exhausted, and winter coming on. Lastly, and worse than all, she was deficient in that spirit of enterprise and energy required to meet the difficulties of her situation. Yet her mental debate was not very long; for all her early impressions and all her religious principles were against the proposed measure. In a few hours, therefore, Sybil's mind was fully made up.

The winter set in very cold. The air was frosty and nipping; snow-clouds darkened the sky. The day on which Sybil was to give her answer to General Brotherton dawned. It was intensely cold. As Sybil arose from her bed, shrinking and shuddering from the biting air, she covered up closely her sleeping boy, saying —

"God bless thee, poor little one! You will freeze if I take you up to-day."

She passed into the parlor, where Katy was attempting to open the shutters. They were so bound with ice and blocked up with snow, that it required considerable effort to push them open; and then the dreary aspect abroad, the ground deeply covered with snow; the sky, gloomily darkened with clouds, was rendered still more dreary by the severely felt privations at home.

"My dear Miss Middleton, you're shivering from head to foot; let me go get your shawl," exclaimed Katy, with chattering teeth.

"Do, Katy. But, Katy, is there no wood left to make a fire?" asked Sybil, shuddering.

"There's one blessed long log left. I going to split it up now. 'Deed and 'deed, Miss Middleton, if I was you, I'd take the child, and I'd go settle down on some o' my relations."

"Without an invitation, and perhaps without a welcome either, Katy?"

"I dunno, I dunno, Miss Sybil! Cross looks don't bite like this cold."

"No, Katy, but worse; one bites the fingers and toes, but the other gnaws at the heart."

Katy made no reply, but went out, and soon returned with her arm full of split wood, of which she made a fire.

"Now, Katy, what have we for breakfast?" inquired Sybil.

"One blessed pint of flour, and one teaspoonful of black tea."

"Then, Katy, get it ready, and we will eat our last meal by our last fire."

The poor meal was scarcely over, and the table removed, before there came a knock at the door, followed by the entrance of General Brotherton, who, taking a seat at the fire, unceremoniously exclaimed —

"Oh! my dear little cousin, this is dreadful weather for traveling; yet we'll have to venture it; for when it moderates, and this snow melts, the roads will be impassable for a fortnight. Come! can you get ready by to-morrow morning?

I wrote a week ago to the old lady, to look for us to-morrow evening."

"My dear cousin," said Sybil, "you must not think me ungrateful, if I decline your kind offer."

"Decline it! Upon what ground? Upon what ground?"

"I am not able to comply with its conditions."

"Which one? which one?"

"That of the divorce."

"Oh! is that all? Yes, you can; nothing is more easy. It is only to apply to the Legislature, and"——

"Understand me, my dear sir. I cannot conscientiously take any steps towards the accomplishment of such a measure," said Sybil, gently.

"Um — hum - m — ah ha! I said so; I knew it; just like all other women — fools! stick to a bad man through thick and thin; and if he runs away, wear the willow fifty years for his sake. But look here, Sybil — my poor Sybil — don't weep; look at your child; look at him, and have a little mercy on his tender frame and his many wants," said the old man, pointing to little Hubert.

Sybil *did* look at her thinly clad and shivering child, and the appeal reached her heart; yet, mastering her rising emotion, she answered —

"I have! I have! I have thought of all that; and yet — and yet I cannot, *indeed* I cannot, do as you recommend."

"Then God help you!" exclaimed the old man, rising in pique; "I have no more to say. Good-morning, my dear."

"Won't you sit longer, cousin?" asked Sybil, timidly.

"No! no, I thank you. I shall be very busy all day to-day. I shall leave to-morrow."

The fire was dying out, and the room was getting chilly, so that Sybil did not press her invitation. She extended her hand cordially to the old man, as she said —

"You will remember, dear General, to get those letters for me."

"Yes, yes; I'll do that," said he. "Good-by, cousin Sybil; farewell, little one," said he, shaking hands with Sybil, and caressing the child.

"Never mind," thought the old gentleman, as he entered his carriage, "I'll let her alone a while, and I'll bet before the month is out she'll be writing to me, revoking her decision."

The old man was gone, the fire had burnt out, and Sybil and her boy were left alone before the cold hearth. Sybil caught up the boy to her bosom, and wept bitterly. Suddenly she thought of the preacher whom she had heard the preceding Sunday. The hopeful and comforting words of his discourse came back to her mind with a soothing influence. They did more; they inspired her with courage and energy.

"Yes," said she aloud, "that minister! why did I not think of him before? I *know* he is a good man, and he will advise me in what manner to set about procuring pupils. I will go to him at once."

CHAPTER X.

THE PASTOR.

MRS. MIDDLETON went to the pastor's house, was shown up into his study, and informed by the servant that Mr. Livingston would be with her in a few minutes. Sybil had changed very much since her first presentation to the reader. Though not yet twenty years old, the rose of youth had faded from her pale cheek; yet her fair complexion — large, clear, blue, serene eyes — her sweet serious lips — her gentle manner — and low sweet voice, and her mourning-dress, rendered her far more interesting than in her days of health and happiness. Sybil wanted self-possession, and she trembled slightly as she entered the pastor's study. The ten minutes, however, that elapsed before his entrance, enabled her to regain composure.

Mr. Livingston, the pastor, now entered. He was a man of about forty years of age, tall, slender, with dark hair and eyes, and strikingly handsome, notwithstanding a pale complexion and hollow cheeks. Mrs. Middleton was reassured by the kindly manner and gentle tones with which this Christian pastor greeted her.

"I hope you will pardon the liberty I take in calling upon you, Mr. Livingston. I am a stranger in this city, and I wish to open a small school, by which to support myself and child; and I have come to-day to solicit your assistance in my project, or at least your advice as to what steps it will be proper to take towards its accomplishment."

"You are a widow, I presume, madam?" said the pastor, glancing at Mrs. Middleton's mourning dress.

"No, sir," murmured Sybil, a burning blush mounting to her brow.

The pastor looked at her in doubt; then said—

"You are probably able to produce good references?"

"Sir?"

"You are provided with testimonials of moral and intellectual fitness for the profession you wish to enter upon?"

"I have no such testimonials, sir, just now; but I hope to receive some in a few days, from my native place."

"They are indispensable to your success, my dear madam, and I trust you will be able to procure them; if you do, I shall take pleasure in rendering all the assistance in my power towards the accomplishment of your object."

A quick flush passed over the pale cheek of Mrs. Middleton. She felt humiliated. She knew that she was suspected. She did *not* know that such was the case with every poor, needy, and friendless woman, especially if she be young, pretty, and a stranger. Sybil arose and took leave. Her parting look of suffering resignation smote upon the heart of the minister. He stepped after her, and said, gently —

"Give me your name and address, madam; I will call and see what can be done in your case to-morrow."

Sybil now recollected, with confusion, that she had not given her name. She did as he requested, and went her way home reassured, thinking —

"I was not mistaken, after all, in Mr. Livingston — such a calm and holy smile — such a sweet, soothing voice — and then his general manner, so gentle, though I saw he did not think justly of me; but my awkwardness and confusion impressed him unfavorably at first."

The next day the minister called. Sybil was in her chamber, putting her boy to sleep, so that the minister sat in her little parlor some ten minutes, before she made her appearance. Mr. Livingston *had* been favorably impressed with Sybil; he was now confirmed in his good opinion by the appearance of her home. There is something about a dwelling, or the furniture of a dwelling, that will impress one favorably, or otherwise, with its occupant. Sybil's little parlor told her story. The furniture was a portion of that brought from Brotherton Hall, telling of decayed gentility. There was the rich old Turkey carpet, somewhat worn, that covered the floor; there were the crimson damask curtains, somewhat faded, that hung from the windows; there were the old-fashioned stuffed chairs — the large, unwieldy sofa — the heavy mahogany tables; and last, and most eloquent, were the fine old family portraits, all choice specimens of art, that hung upon the walls. There was a portrait of old Mrs. Brotherton, of Sybil's father and mother, and one of Sybil herself. One very characteristic thing I neglected to mention. It was three hanging shelves, containing Sybil's library of novels and romances. The observant eye of the pastor noted and drew conclusions from everything; but the portrait of Sybil in her blooming happy girlhood, arrested and fixed his attention. He was gazing upon it, in deep thought, when Mrs. Middleton came in.

"My dear Mrs. Middleton," said he, turning to meet her, "I must beg your confidence; you have told me that you are distressed; I see that you are reduced. I wish to devote my poor energies to your service; but, in order to serve you effectually, I would know more of your circumstances and expectations."

Sybil looked in his face. The noble frankness of the expression inspired her with confidence. She thanked him, and, with a flushed cheek and averted eye, she told her story. The minister listened with deep attention, and at the close of her narration he sought to direct her attention to the Great Source of strength and joy. Feeling her religious sympathies drawn out, Sybil related the emotion she had felt upon the receipt of her last letter, the whirlwind of anger that had shaken her soul, her subsequent alarm and repentance, and the peace and hope that had filled her bosom since. To this *naïve* confession the pastor listened with deep interest; for by that glimpse into the soul of Sybil he recognised a nature capable of the highest religious and intellectual culture, and one therefore likely to be refined in the seven times heated furnace of affliction. Moral philosophy was the pastor's favorite study; and men and women, with their trials and temptations, were the books he read upon the subject. The refined, the strong, the tempted and struggling soul of Sybil Middleton attracted him forcibly, and he resolved to watch, to shield, and strengthen it in its contest. But, of that, more by and by. He did not for a moment lose sight of the immediate object of his visit — the temporal welfare of his intended *protegée*. He discovered Sybil's musical proficiency, and advised her to commence by instructing a few young ladies in that accomplishment, and volunteered to go among his parishioners, and seek out pupils for her. Mrs. Middleton expressed her gratitude, and the pastor arose to take leave. His eyes fell upon Sybil's bookshelves, filled with romances, and a slight smile curled his lip, as he asked —

"Is this your favorite reading, Mrs. Middleton?"

"In my days of ease and cheerfulness I used to delight in these books," answered Sybil; "but now "——

"But now you require the most precious thoughts of the most holy writers to comfort and sustain you — books that you can feed upon. Shall I send you some such?"

"If you please, Mr. Livingston; I shall be very grateful. But, indeed, you are too kind to me — to me, who have no claim upon you, or any one else."

"Pardon me; you *have* a claim upon me, and a claim upon society; and the claim is mutual. Society demands of you, that you cultivate all your natural gifts to the utmost, and use them for its benefit. You, then, have a right to demand of society, *happiness.*"

The minister took leave, and the same day went about among the members of his congregation to solicit pupils for his new *protegée.* The Rev. Stephen Livingston was more than popular among his parishioners; he had a rising name, and they were proud of him. Any enterprise, therefore, favored by their pastor, was very likely to be highly successful. Mr. Livingston's *protegée* was enthusiastically taken up and excessively patronized by his congregation. A class of fifteen pupils was soon made up for Mrs. Middleton. Many of them, at Mr. Livingston's instance, paid in advance; and in that way Sybil's immediate wants were relieved. From this time, the light of hope sparkled again in the eyes of Sybil, the rose of health bloomed again on her cheeks. Her new profession introduced her among an intelligent and cultivated circle of acquaintances, some of whom, who were not too aristocratic to notice their children's teacher, eventually became warm friends. Mrs. Middleton became deeply yet healthfully interested in the progress of her pupils; and when her list of fifteen increased to thirty, nearly all her time in the day was taken up in attending upon them. The day would thus pass quickly and pleasantly away; for my heroine, reader, was of a cheerful and grateful temper, and did not call her daily occupation *toil*, nor her interest in it *anxiety*. Then upon her return home in the evening, she would find a blazing fire, and tea prepared in her little parlor, and perhaps a new book left by the pastor, awaiting her. When the weather would permit, little Hubert would be at the gate waiting, and would totter forth to meet her. At such times, the mother's heart would bound to meet her boy, and, catching him up in her arms, she would hurry into the house, and, sitting down, would strain him to her bosom, covering him with kisses the while. Katy, since she was no longer pinched with hunger or chilled with cold, was as blithe as a bird, and sung at her work all day long; while old Broom, who had run his visit into a permanent stay, employed himself in sawing and packing away wood for the winter's use; in clearing up the garden, which he meant to put under cultivation in the spring; and in attending to little Hubert.

CHAPTER XI.

SYBIL A WIDOW.

ONE cold, damp evening, near the spring, Sybil returned home later than usual. It had been drizzling all day long, and towards evening the rain had fallen in torrents. Sybil had remained with the pupil whom she had last visited until near dark, hoping that the rain would cease. At last, borrowing an umbrella, she set out for home. How cheerful looked her little cottage, with the lights gleaming through its parlor windows! She entered the house, and, throwing aside her cloak and hood, looked around for little Hubert. Not seeing him, she passed into her chamber, where he lay asleep; kissing him softly, and murmuring a blessing, she returned to the little parlor. Everything was comfortable there; the wood fire was blazing cheerfully; the tea-table was set, and Sybil's work-stand and basket placed in the corner, with her rocking-chair and footstool near it. Sybil sat down at her work-stand, while Katy brought in tea.

"The parson has been here, ma'am," said Katy; "waited for you a good while; just gone away; left this book for you in your work-basket."

Sybil took up the book, murmuring to herself—

"'Paley'; oh! Mr. Livingston is so kind! No one was ever so kind to me before, except my poor old grandmother. But what is this, Katy?" said she, about taking up a packet directed, in a strange hand, to herself, and bearing a ship stamp; "who left this?"

"That! Yes, ma'am; he brought that, too, from the pos' office for you."

Sybil tore off the envelope. It was a London paper. She unfolded it, and read with astonishment and grief the following notice, to which her attention was directed by a couple of pen strokes:

"DIED, at his residence in Portman Square, on the thirtieth of October, Harold Preble Middleton, son of the Hon. Fenton Preble Middleton, and grandson of the Right Hon. the Earl of Mainwaring."

The paper dropped from her hands, and Sybil fell into thought. She did not reflect upon the man who had oppressed, deserted, slandered her; she thought only of the lover of her youth, the father of her child, and her tears began to flow faster than she could wipe them away.

"Well, I declare, Mrs. Middleton," said Katy, coming in, "you have not touched a mouthful of supper. I took such pains with them sponge cakes, too; and the tea is best 'perial."

"You may take the table away, Katy," said Sybil, and, arising and passing into her chamber, she fell weeping upon the crib of her child.

CHAPTER XII.

GENERAL AND MRS. BROTHERTON.

TO say that Sybil was the "inconsolable" widow of a man whom she had married upon a slight and insufficient acquaintance; who had remained with her comparatively but a short time; who had abused her even unto personal violence; who had forsaken her at her utmost need; aspersed her character, and disowned her child — to say this would be an incredible libel on her sanity. "Some natural tears she shed, but wiped them soon." She remained at home a fortnight, and occupied herself with making up her mourning, without thinking of the necessity of sending notes of explanation to her patrons, who were left by that omission to conjecture the cause of her protracted absence from her pupils. These conjectures at length reached the ears of the pastor, and he resolved to call and see Mrs. Middleton. He found Sybil calmly at work with her needle, while her little boy played upon the carpet. No change in Sybil's looks warned him of what had occurred, so he said to her playfully —

"My dear Mrs. Middleton, I have resolved myself into a committee of inquiry, to ascertain the cause or causes of your self-immersement."

In their lively moments, Sybil had always answered his smiles with smiling, and his quibs with quiddities, but now her grave countenance seemed to rebuke his jesting. Requesting him to be seated, she arose from her chair, and, taking from her writing-desk the London paper, put it into his hands, and, pointing to the obituary notice, said, while the tears arose to her eyes —

"The knowledge of *that event* has kept me at home for some time past. Will you please inform my patrons of it?"

Her large, tender eyes were raised to the pastor's face as she spoke, and she observed with surprise and displeasure the sudden, the involuntary flush of — *something* that lighted up the pastor's face as he read. Well! I own it; for my part, I *do* "expect perfection from human beings," at least from some of us, and especially from Christian ministers; and I feel humiliated to be obliged to acknowledge the existence of a single human weakness in Mr. Livingston; but so it was, the Rev. Stephen Livingston, the fervent Christian, the beloved pastor, the rising divine, had not lately, with his *whole soul,* worshiped one God, but in the temple of his heart *one niche* was occupied by an idol. Little did he suspect this, however, until, in perusing the paragraph, he discovered the real nature of his regard for Sybil, by the sudden recollection of the possibility of its gratification. Reproaching himself immediately and bitterly for this feeling, he returned the paper to Sybil, saying coldly, as he arose to take leave —

"Mrs. Middleton, you may, and I hope will, command my services in this distressing affair, whenever they may be required."

Sybil thanked him, and returned his cold " Good-evening, madam," with a distant " Good-night, sir."

"And now," thought the pastor, as he turned from the door, " I do not see that I have effaced *one* error of sinful exultation, by another error of studied coldness. Poor child! at the very moment that she required consolation, advice, and assistance, to leave her so abruptly, without offering a single word of comfort. I must certainly see her again soon, and make amends for this."

Mrs. Middleton also indulged in a soliloquy to this effect — " I am afraid, after all, that I have a very bad, or at least a very conceited mind ; to think that I should be so vain as to suppose that Mr. Livingston was — that he felt — that the pastor thought" — Sybil durst not finish the sentence, even mentally, but, with a feeling of self-abasement, endeavored to force her thoughts from the subject, after saying to herself —

"Yes, yes; I have done the good pastor foul wrong by my vain suspicions. Well, well; I will be more reasonable when he comes again, if, indeed, he *ever* comes, after my cold ingratitude."

The next day the pastor called with more *friendly* offers of assistance, and his visit passed off in the easy manner of their first acquaintance. At his suggestion, Sybil resolved to do many things, very necessary to be done, but which, with her limited knowledge of life, she would not else have thought of doing. For instance, the obituary notice was sent to some of the Baltimore papers; a letter was written to General Brotherton, informing him of her widowhood; and another letter was written to the Earl of Mainwaring, inquiring the particulars of Mr. Middleton's decease. Having assisted Sybil in all these matters, Mr. Livingston refrained from visiting her again. It was now, by missing it, that Sybil began to estimate the society of the pastor at its full value; she also divined the cause of his absence, though no word or glance had hinted it — such is the mental free-masonry of affection.

A few weeks after this, when the spring had well opened, Sybil received a visit from General and Mrs. Brotherton. They had come to renew their generous proposal to Sybil, and, in the event of her rejecting it, to invite her to pass the first year of her widowhood at Brotherton Hall. In thinking of Mrs. General Brotherton, and in hearing her called by the General "the old lady," and "the old wife," and "my old lady," Sybil had pictured to herself a venerable woman, not unlike her departed grandmother. What was her surprise, then, when the General introduced her to a handsome, fashionable-looking Frenchwoman, really forty-eight, but apparently about thirty-five years of age. Sybil had heard, it is true, that General Brotherton, during his service in the old French war, had been taken prisoner, and, during his captivity, had fallen in love with and married the daughter of a French officer, but she had lately forgotten it. General and Mrs. Brotherton remained in Baltimore a fortnight, and, during that time, the old proposition to Sybil was renewed. As there now existed no obstacle to its acceptance, Sybil gratefully acceded to it, and began making active preparations for a removal to Brotherton Hall, the General superintending the packing *up* and *off* of the furniture, while Madame busied herself among milliners and mantua-makers, compelling Sybil to go with her on all her excursions. Though no two people could be more opposite in temper than the lively Frenchwoman and the thoughful Sybil, yet (for this very reason, perhaps) they were strongly attached to each other. Sybil had parted with all her pupils, and taken leave of all her friends, and so she felt and looked very serious as she entered the carriage with General and Mrs. Brotherton, on the morning of her departure; so that Madame said to her —

"Come! ma belle, you put on a look of fortitude quite gratuitous, under the circumstances; for really, I cannot see that it requires so much moral courage to reconcile you to a black dress, when it becomes you so extremely well. If *I*, now, with my dark complexion, were compelled to make myself hideous in widow's weeds, it might be a matter of regret; but *you* — a fine girl like you — could not wear a more becoming color; therefore, leave that look of resignation, for I shall neither pity nor praise you on account of it."

Sybil raised her eyes to the face of Mrs. Brotherton in simple wonder.

"Ah! ah! *mignonne*," exclaimed Madame. "Your eyes are quite large enough, and very beautiful, just as they are; do not try to stretch them any larger; for, *en verité*, I think your look of wonder even less attractive than your look of martyrdom."

"She's not mad, cousin Sybil; at least, not

raving mad, although you may fear it. I assure you there is no danger. Madame is a harmless lunatic," said the General, seriously.

Sybil laughed, in spite of herself. The object of her two relatives was effected; they had rallied her into cheerfulness. It was in May. It was late at night, and the full moon was shining brightly when they arrived at Brotherton Hall, and Sybil re-entered the home of her childhood.

CHAPTER XIII.

SYBIL'S DREAM OF HAPPINESS.

A YEAR had passed since the arrival of Mrs. Middleton and her child at Brotherton Hall — a year during which she had won the affection of her relatives, who esteemed her as a daughter — a year dotted with a few bright days, the occasions upon which her sometime pastor had blessed Brotherton Hall with his visits.

Her letter to the Earl of Mainwaring had not been answered; but then a voyage across the Atlantic, fifty years ago, was not the afternoon excursion that it is now; so that Sybil waited five or six months without anxiety. At the end of that time, she had written again, and, to insure the safe delivery of her letter at its destination, she had enclosed it to the American Minister at the Court of St. James. She was now expecting an answer to this last letter. The spring opened beautifully. The sunshine abroad was not more bright, warm, and genial, than the sunshine of the breast enjoyed by Sybil Middleton. At no period of her short life had Sybil been so happy. By a judicious attention to the laws of physiology, her early constitutional tendency to consumption had been conquered. By free exercise in the open air, and frequent bathing, she had attained high health; and, during the course of her acquaintance with Mr. Livingston, her intellectual faculties had become greatly unfolded; and now Sybil Middleton, in the full development and high enjoyment of mental, moral, and physical life, dreamed that she was about to attain the acme of human happiness; for one who had assisted her in difficulty, advised her in prosperity, sympathized with her in sorrow — one who had developed and cultivated her intellect, enlarged and elevated her moral sense, enlightened and exalted her Christian faith — one whom she loved and worshiped next to God himself — had received her promise to become his wife. It was with the candor of pure affection that Sybil expressed the full joy she felt in giving him her hand. It is true that, for some months past, Sybil had expected this proposal; yet, now that it had been made, she could scarcely believe in the reality of her happiness. That Livingston, upon whose words she had hung with such deep joy — that he from whose instructions she had derived such strength and comfort — he upon whom she constantly depended for guidance — he whom she revered and honored first upon earth, and whom she had lately grown to love with the whole strength of her earnest soul — that he should take her to his bosom, to pass her whole life with him, to bear his honored name, to share his blessed labors — oh! this seemed a happiness too full for earth, and Sybil trembled amidst her joy, as the day of their marriage drew near.

"In one short week, my own dear Sybil!—in one short week we meet again, to part no more on earth. Oh! the joy, the joy to feel that this is our last brief separation! for I have grieved to leave you, even for a few days, my Sybil!" exclaimed Mr. Livingston, as he folded his betrothed bride to his bosom.

"Oh! yes, in one week more," murmured Sybil; "yet, ah! my own love, I grow superstitious, and tremble lest this joy be too full to last."

She raised her head from his bosom, and looked into his face; their eyes met in a long, full, earnest gaze; again he pressed her to his bosom in a silent embrace. Ah! if they could have died in that embrace! They parted.

CHAPTER XIV.

THE AWAKENING.

MR. LIVINGSTON, on his arrival at the parsonage late that night, found letters awaiting him. The first that arrested his attention bore a foreign mark; it was evidently from an acquaintance of his in London, and in answer to a letter of inquiry, written on the part of Mrs. Middleton. He took it up, opened the seal, and began to read. Did a basilisk blast his sight? Had he plucked up a mandrake to drive him mad? The paper fell from his cold hands; dashing his clenched fists against his burning brow, he groaned out—

"My God! my God! This is too much for humanity to bear! Let me die now!"

He rushed out into the air, and up and down, through the cool streets he walked, without calming the fever of his blood, or cooling the fire in his brain — up and down through the silent streets, muttering half-smothered words of despair and grief — up and down through the dark streets, with a strange light gleaming in his eyes, until morning dawned; then hurrying to his house, he shut himself up in his study, saying —

"No, no; I must not see her in this state of mind! I must strive to conquer this. Good God! shall I, who pretend to strengthen and console others, go mad, or die myself?"

When the sun arose, and shone into the study of the pastor, its beams fell upon a face that seemed to have grown old in a night. He was sitting at a little table facing the window; his face was pale and haggard, his eyes hollow, his gaze strained upon a text in the open Bible before him, his thoughts concentrated upon a point — long he remained so; at length his head drooped upon the book — he prayed; it was the first time he had dared to pray since the opening of the fatal letter; he was strengthened; he became composed — though all day long he remained in his study without refreshment, reading, praying, and meditating — though all night long he kept a vigil there, yet upon the following day, which was Sunday, he preached with his usual power and perspicuity. It is true that his congregation were shocked at his haggard countenance and shaking frame, and many of them made anxious inquiries concerning his health. Their pastor confessed that he was not well, and finally succeeded in escaping from his officious friends, and regaining the privacy of his home. Early on Monday morning, the pastor arose, and, having saddled his horse himself, mounted, and took his way towards Brotherton Hall. He was again changed. Not a vestige of emotion was visible in his face or manner. His countenance was sorrowful, but calm, resolute, and still. His manner gentle and serious, yet determined.

That day Sybil was sitting alone, at work, singing in the overflowing joy of her heart. The little boy was trundling a hoop in the yard, and ever and anon, his merry laugh and shout came in at the open windows. General and Mrs. Brotherton were out taking a ride. Presently, there was a sound of a horse's feet in the yard, a familiar foot-step in the hall, a hand upon the lock, and Mr. Livingston stood before Sybil. His face was pale, and wore the impress of desperate sorrow, yet inflexible resolution.

Sybil had sprung to meet him, yet stood transfixed by his looks.

"Good heavens, dearest! what is the matter? Has anything happened?" exclaimed she.

"Sit down, Sybil," said he, gravely; at the same time taking a seat himself.

"Yes — I will — but, oh! indeed something *has* happened — I see it by your looks. Dear love, what *can* it be?" exclaimed Sybil, anxiously.

"Yes, Sybil, something *has* happened — something to change the whole current of our future lives. You are growing pale, Sybil; summon all your Christian fortitude, or, if your strength fail, call on Him who giveth freely. I have received a letter from my London correspondent on the subject upon which I wrote to him months ago— you remember" ——

"Yes! yes! well? well?"——

"Well, Sybil!—my poor Sybil, we have been laboring under a fatal mistake—your husband is living!" Sybil fell back in her chair, deadly pale and faint. Mr. Livingston poured out and handed her a glass of water, which, when she had drank, she murmured—

"It is over—it is over—that happy dream."

Deceived by her quietness, the pastor went on to say—

"This was the way in which the mistake originated, Mrs. Middleton" ——

"You need not tell me! It is of no use! We do not care to know how the poison was distilled that has sapped our lives! We do not inquire where the dagger was wrought that is sheathed in our hearts"——

"Sybil! Sybil!—Oh, Heaven support her—her hands are icy cold—her breath comes thick and short. Sybil!—Oh! my poor Sybil—bear up under this; be resigned to the will of Heaven."

"Commonplace! commonplace! You'd say the same to a mother whose only child was about to be hung! 'Be resigned!' 'Bear up!' And have I *not* borne up? Have I *not* been resigned? *I*, that have suffered as no one ever suffered before me! *I*, that have been tried as no one ever was tried before me! Resignation! fortitude! What have they done for me, but to provoke upon my head a reiteration of trial, as if Heaven were making the experiment of how much sorrow a human being could bear without going mad!"

"Now, may Heaven forgive your wild words, Sybil! Oh, Sybil! suffer me to pray with you, as in days past!"

"Pray!" exclaimed she, bitterly; "to whom, and for what? *Pray!* I've prayed all my life; and here I sit, a tortured, a blighted, a miserable woman! I would I were annihilated!"

"Oh! Sybil, if this were the *only* life, *still* you would have no excuse for such a frantic arraingment of Providence. But, oh! bethink you, this dark, this thorny, this sorrowful road, if we tread it firmly and patiently, will lead us to"——

"'Another and a happier world,' perhaps. I know nothing of it! I do not see it! I do not hear it! Away with it! I will none of it! — Give me — oh! give me happiness in *this* world, that I know." And Sybil, extending her arms pleadingly towards her lover, burst into tears. Struggling with a powerful emotion, the pastor turned abruptly, and walked to a window, at the opposite end of the room, where he remained a long time, apparently gazing out upon the landscape.

Laughing, jesting, and joyous, General Brotherton and his wife now entered the room, from their drive. Sybil slipped out, and fled to her chamber to conceal her emotion, while the pastor turned tranquilly to meet them.

Very early on the next morning, Mr. Livingston descended to the parlor. He was to leave Brotherton Hall after the family breakfast — to leave it with the probability of never returning — yet he resolved, before going, to put in execution a plan which he had matured during the night. He had been very much shaken by the despair of Sybil. He knew her disposition better than she knew herself. He knew that there could be no risk in the plan he resolved to propose, in order to rouse all the energy of her soul, to throw off the weight of her sorrow. Through all this seeming stoicism, the pastor ever felt the wound that was festering in his own heart. The pastor had not been down many minutes, before Sybil entered. She was very, very pale, gentle, and subdued. Sinking, trembling, in a chair, she said, in a low, sad voice —

"Give me the letter now, my friend; I can read it now."

The pastor placed it in her hands. She read as follows:

"My Dear Friend: I have made inquiries concerning the person of whom you wrote me. The obituary notice in the London paper referred to the honorable Harold Preble Middleton, the grandson of the Earl of Mainwaring, a gentleman who has never left England, and who, besides, has left a widow and children in Portman Square. I have since learned that there is a relative of the family, bearing the same name, who spent three years in America. This person is represented to be a sort of genteel loafer, or aristocratic vagabond, who spends his time in 'going to and fro on the earth, and passing up and down in it;' a sort of amateur artist, and is now at Rome, studying the old masterpieces of painting. With him is an Italian woman, who passes for his wife — one Inez or Inice di Silva."

The letter was long, but it here left the subject of so much interest to Sybil; so, folding it up slowly and calmly, she returned it to Livingston. Sybil was composed, but it was the composure of despair, the quiet of weakness — the feebleness of nature was upon her. Her heart seemed melting, dying in her bosom; and indeed she thought, and welcomed the thought, that this weakness was unto death. The pastor saw this, and felt the urgent necessity of rousing her.

"I am much relieved to see you have regained composure, dear Sybil."

"Yes — I have regained composure " — said she, sighing. "But, oh! my dear friend, I have lost your good opinion — I know it — I feel it; through the ravings of my despair, I have lost your esteem for ever."

"No, dear Sybil, my esteem for you remains undiminished; I never supposed you to be an angel, and I am not surprised to find you a woman."

"But you were so firm, so self-possessed, so calm."

"Yes, Sybil, after two nights of moral tempest; and my calmness was perhaps as much the effect of exhausted nature, as of reason or religion. We have both sinned, Sybil, not *hitherto* in our attachment — for that was involuntary, inevitable — but in the terrible arraignment of Providence of which we have both been guilty."

"Yes, yes. Oh! I feel that," said Sybil. "It is well for us, indeed, that our Father in Heaven is so long-suffering and patient with us. Listen, my friend; when I fled to my chamber last evening, I was mad! The very elements of my being were broken up — all was storm, confusion, chaos! and this storm raged through my soul until it exhausted my strength. I felt as though the very earth had rolled from beneath my feet, and I had forfeited my claim upon Heaven. Eternal night seemed to have fallen upon my soul; I was desolate, forsaken, *cursed*. I was mad! I was tempted! The thought of self-destruction flashed into my mind, and I said, I will leave life, I will fly to death; and with the sophistry of passion I added, I shall not be as a rebellious subject, rushing unbidden into the presence of his king — no, no, but as a tempest-driven child, flying for refuge to the bosom of her Father. I started up, my grasp was upon the lock of the door, when a gentle hand, a weak infant's hand, held me back. I turned, and little Hubert was standing by me, looking with wonder and grief upon me — while he murmured, '*I* love you, mamma.' Oh! my friend, can you understand the revulsion of feeling that overpowered me? I sank down where I was, and, folding the babe to my bosom, I wept; and as my emotion subsided, I became penetrated with a sense of my ingratitude and sin, and I prayed; but oh! my friend, *before* I prayed, simultaneously with the first dawning of penitence came a sense of forgiveness. God meets us more than half way with pardon; he does not wait for the bended knee; he does not stay for the forming prayer; he meets the first impulse of penitence with forgiveness. I do not pretend to account for the existence of suffering, I do not clearly comprehend the use of trial, but I know that God is good; I feel that God is love; I believe that we are not tortured in vain. But I am an egotist— I have talked too long; yet you have been in some sort my father confessor, Livingston," added she, with a sorrowful attempt to smile. The short-lived animation that had borne her through this speech was fast dying away.

"No, dear Sybil, you have given me comfort," replied the pastor.

He still called her "dear Sybil," for he could not bring himself to address the failing, fainting woman before him, in any but the language of tenderness. She had relapsed into a fearful apathy — her form was still as death — her face was ashy pale even to her lips — the very torpor of despair seemed to have stupefied her — the very elements of existence seemed resolving into dissolution. The pastor saw this with alarm, and hastened to rouse her attention by the proposal of his plan.

"Listen to me, dear Sybil; there is hope for us yet."

"Hope!" echoed Sybil, unconsciously.

"Yes, hope. Attend to me, dear Sybil, if you please. You remember the proposition made to you by General Brotherton about two years ago — you *remember*, Sybil?"

"Yes," said Sybil, absently.

"When General Brotherton is informed of the contents of this letter, that proposition will be renewed. Do you not think so?"

"Possibly," replied Sybil, indifferently.

"*Probably,* nay, certainly. What if you were to accept the conditions, and free yourself?"

Starting, half raising herself, bending forward, while the light brightened in her eyes and the color warmed in her cheek, she exclaimed —

"Mr. Livingston, my friend, do *you* advise me to this?"

"Nay, Sybil — I advise you to nothing. This is a matter, above all others, upon which you must not take advice; but I *do* say to you, that it is worth investigation; and I promise, that if, after you shall have examined the subject by the light of the Holy Scriptures, with the aid of sincere prayer, you may religiously as well as legally free yourself, and enter a second engagement, I will then entreat you to bless me with your hand."

"But," said Sybil, reviving, "even if our own consciences were satisfied, such a marriage might impair your usefulness."

"It might secure our happiness."

"No! as Heaven hears me," exclaimed Sybil, warmly, "I would not purchase happiness, *even for you*, at the price of the faintest shadow upon your Christian character."

"Dismiss that from your mind, Sybil. Let us

strive to understand the will of God. Let us strive to do that which is right in the sight of God, and leave the consequences with Him."

"Then tell me what is right, my own dear guide and mentor. I do not wish to go beyond you for direction in this difficulty. I am sure you know what is right, for you have seemed to stand between my God and myself, interpreting his will to me."

"No, Sybil! my gentle one, this is between God and your own conscience; it would be sacrilege to interfere. You must 'tread the wine press alone,' looking to Him for fortitude who entered it *alone* before you."

"Alas! alas! and I have no father or mother to advise with me, no brother or sister to comfort me, no friend when you are gone to sympathize with me."

"Dear Sybil, you are of all persons the best fitted to judge of your own case, by the light of religion; no one knows the circumstances as you know them."

"I am very well aware that it is considered extremely ill-natured to intrude upon lovers; but when they choose the family breakfast room, early in the morning, for their *tête-à-tête*, and less happy folks are hungry, how can it be avoided?" exclaimed the jovial old General, as he bustled into the room.

How this merriment jarred upon the excited nerves of Sybil!

"When I was wooing, we used to take woodland walks on such fine spring mornings as this. Ask Madame — here she comes. I'm telling these transported people, Gabrielle, when you and I were transcendentalated, we did not stay about the house putting sensible people to inconvenience by taking possession of their breakfast room, keeping them from their chocolate. No; when *we* were etherealized, and left eating and drinking to people that were 'of the earth earthy,' we rehearsed our dreams and visions 'amid the vasty solitudes of nature,' as cousin

Sybil's books call mountains and forests. Come! old lady," added he, patting his wife affectionately on the shoulder, "make them stir about — stir about. As I have been shooting at water fowl and not at hearts, this morning, I am smitten with a rather exacting affection for coffee and toast."

The general had lately affected to call his wife "old lady," — a *sobriquet* which the pretty Frenchwoman never failed to receive with a toss of the head, at once haughty, petulant, and graceful, which shook down her ringlets in the most becoming fall.

Breakfast was served; and immediately after it was removed, the pastor arose to take leave. He shook hands with Mrs. Brotherton, with the General, and approached Sybil with a sinking, dying heart — with a reeling brain. Well he knew that this was the last, last time he should ever behold her. Truly he felt that he should never, *never* again, see her face, hear her voice, touch her hand — the woman towards whom his whole being tended with a force, by an attraction, almost impossible to be checked. His heart sank, his brain reeled, his voice quivered, yet his words were cold.

"Mrs. Middleton, farewell."

"Good-by," said Sybil, as her cold hand fell heavily from his grasp.

That cold, conventional leave-taking, amid the merry group! and with their bursting hearts! Well, perhaps it was better.

"'*Mrs. Middleton!*' Well, I call Venus, Cupid, and Psyche, and all the Muses and Graces, to witness that I never called the old lady by any name than 'Flower,' 'Star,' 'Pearl,' 'Angel,' 'Seraph,' or '*Gabrielle,*' that meant each and all, from the moment of our engagement until some three or four weeks after marriage!"

Livingston was gone.

"Why, cousin Sybil, what do you intend to do with such an icicle as that? Decidedly, that man has mistaken his vocation. He was intended for a monk. Sybil! Heavens! What is the matter? Wife! come here; she's ill — she's got an inflammation on the brain — her hands are cold as ice, her head as hot as fire — her eyes are wild. Sybil! speak to your old cousin; how do you feel?"

"What is Good? What is Evil? Where is God?" asked Sybil, wildly.

"Oh; my good gracious; she's mad, raving mad. Old lady, I say! All owing to that strong coffee — destroyed her nervous system. All owing to coffee and novels — drinking strong coffee and eating — I mean *reading* — novels, I know."

"You know nothing about it. Leave the room, General — you're like a bear nursing a baby," said Mrs. Brotherton, coming in.

"Yes; but Gabe — I mean *old lady*," amended the General, spitefully — "she's very ill, I tell you."

"She is not. It is a rush of blood to the brain — nothing more. Leave her to me."

The General left the room, grumbling, " she 's *my* cousin, Gabrielle — not yours."

Madam looked after him with a fond, quizzing smile. She understood the *pathology* and treatment of overwrought passion as well as a Parisian doctor. Delicately refraining from expressing any surprise, or asking any questions, she applied the necessary remedies, and soon restored her patient to composure.

Livingston had succeeded, by an almost superhuman exertion of will, in subduing all outward demonstrations of emotion while in the presence of Sybil. Leaving Brotherton Hall, he spurred his horse into a furious gallop, as though he would ride away from himself, or win the race of sorrow; and rustics, who saw him shoot past like an arrow, surmised that he carried an express. Then, again, he would permit his horse to fall into a slow walk, as though he were pursuing a journey without object or aim; and those who knew his person, might have conjectured that he was meditating his next Sabbath's discourse. He was tempted — for he knew that it was with himself — *himself* — that this question rested at last. He knew that the woman whose mind he had developed, whose heart was all his own, over whom he possessed unbounded influence, who never questioned his rectitude of principle, who seldom exerted her own moral agency, if *he* were at hand to decide for her — he felt that this woman could not fail to be won by his arguments to any course he should point out to her; and he felt that he was responsible not only for his own moral welfare, but for hers also — and he *loved* her moral welfare, above all things he loved that, and he regretted the feminine softness of character, that while it made her so sweetly attractive, left her so much at his disposal; and he wished that corrected, and he knew that this trial would effect its cure, by calling out all the latent energies of her really strong soul, by arousing the sleeping strength of her pure moral sense; and he had no fears for the result; he knew the features of her mind, as a mother knows the face of her child; he knew that she would suffer, struggle, but *overcome*. And he knew that her soul would come out from this struggle, pure as gold from the furnace, strong as steel from the tempering, healthful as a young giant from the wrestle. But, then, to lose her — *to lose her!* Oh! these three words expressed for him the very alpha and omega, the *all* of mortal agony — and, at the thought, he would feel exasperated to spurn away all his earthly usefulness and interests, to forego all his heavenly hopes and aspirations, to possess her — and *would* have done so, but for the *right-directed will*, the calm, the inflexible, the unchanged, the immutable will — the regal will — that sat restraining, directing, governing, subduing, this revolt of the passions, like an upright judge amid an excited populace.

The pastor reached home, and commenced preparations to remove to the South. And thus it is — whenever two people are disappointed in love, the man goes away somewhere, flies to the North or the South Pole, or makes a balloon voyage to spend a winter in the moon, and speedily effaces old impressions by new ones — while the woman, poor thing, is left to brood over her disappointment, amid the very ruins of her tumbled-down castle from the air, surrounded by all the associations of her past joy — taking the same walks, and missing *one* from her side — sitting in the same parlor, at the same hour, logically looking for the same form, listening for the same voice, "waiting for the steps that come not back." Decidedly, she would break her heart, but that some old aunty reminds her that men are not worth breaking hearts for; and, *besides*, broken hearts have gone out of fashion, and women don't like to be unfashionable.

CHAPTER XV.

THE STRUGGLE.

BUT Sybil, poor Sybil, with her strong affections, her fervent aspirations after right, her feebleness of will, her nervous temperament, and her terrible trial!

When General Brotherton had read the letter that had been silently placed in his hands by Livingston at leaving, the old gentleman's rage exploded and scattered consternation throughout the house. You would have supposed, to have heard him, that he considered the continued existence of Middleton as the very climax of his crimes. If he ever dared to set foot in America, he would hang him up with his own hands, as he would a thieving cur. He wouldn't wait for that — he'd go to Rome, old as he was, *that* he would, and shoot the fellow like a mad dog. And the old gentleman drove the dogs from the room, kicked the cat, scolded the servants, and frightened the child, by way of convincing people that he meant what he said.

After a few days, having reconsidered the subject of setting Providence right in this matter of life and death, General Brotherton renewed his former proposition, and pressed Sybil to its adoption — using all the arguments that his clear, logical, worldly view of the affair could suggest. Sybil, whom the surges of emotion, that had swept over her, had left quiet and weak, replied, that she would *think* of it.

"She will 'think of it.' Gabrielle! do you hear? She 'will think of it;' that's a great point gained. It's easy to perceive that her desire for the crown of martyrdom is considerably diminished. I should judge the parson had set her right upon some points of Christian doctrine."

And Sybil did think of it — until her brain reeled and her reason tottered. She did not examine the moral and legal authorities upon the subject, for she did not possess a logical mind, and she said, properly enough, "They will only confuse my mind with their arguments and counter arguments, for half the time they are more desirous to conquer in controversy, than to find truth; but I will go to the fount of light and truth — I will go to the Bible;" and she went to the Bible, and she searched with care, with eagerness, with breathless avidity, *with an earnest desire to find that which she sought* — Christian permission to free herself; and she found that there is but one cause for which a man may divorce his wife, and *no cause, none*, for which a woman may divorce her husband and marry again. There is something in Bible truth that heals while it probes, that strengthens while it chastises. He who laid down this seemingly partial law understood the hearts of women, and knew the comparatively spiritual nature of their affections. He who delivered this stringent command was himself steeped to the lips in suffering, was himself "tempted in all things *as we are.*" Never before had Sybil so *sympathized* (thus to speak) with the Saviour's sufferings, never had she *so* realized the Saviour's temptations, never had she so received the great lesson of the Saviour's life and death, as now, when, "searching the Scriptures" in sorrow and temptation, and in the tenderness of her melted heart, she breathed forth —

"Not all thy promises, oh! Saviour, affect me so much as thy example and thy sufferings. I will bear my cross, even so, Sufferer and Saviour, for it was thy way."

All emotion, even religious emotion, is shortlived, and not to be trusted. The only permanent safety is in a clear conception of duty, and a resolute determination to act up to it, looking to God for strength. So true is this, that through all their teaching, the Saviour and his Apostles seldom or never appeal to passion or imagination — generally to reason.

Sybil's religious enthusiasm subsided, and then came the temptation in its might — the temptation of a lifetime, the trial of principle, the test of faith, the crisis of character — the point upon which all that could blind to right, all that could tempt to evil, were brought to a focus. To every one who has passed unsullied through the lesser temptations of this world, to every one upon whom the common trials of life have had little influence, to every one who has attained a certain moral point of elevation, there comes once in life one trial of pre-eminent strength, one temptation of almost irresistible might, one test of infallible truth — a temptation, through the most powerful passion of the soul, of the weakest point in the character. This touchstone may be applied in youth, in mid-life, or in age; and the result is almost invariably *final*, giving the bent to character for time and for eternity. To one whose besetting sin is *avarice*, this test may come in the shape of some rare chance to secure a great pecuniary profit, at the cost of a slight departure from rectitude; and it may come in a time of great penury and severe privation, and it may offer affluence at the price of integrity. How severe his struggle then! Will he stop to inquire, "What shall it profit a man, if he gain the whole world, and lose his own soul?" To one of a higher grade, for whom wealth has but little attraction, but to whom the applause of men is as the breath of life, it may come, this touchstone, in the form of some golden opportunity of securing popular favor by a slight deviation from the straight line of duty — as when some great statesman, whose popularity is fluctuating, is tempted of his ambition to engage in some popular but unholy cause; it may come when his favor with men is at the lowest ebb, and it may place within his reach the very prize of his life-long hopes, the very god of his life-long aspirations — requiring of him only to overleap some obstacle of duty to reach it, to let fall some principle of justice to grasp it. Will he, the tempted, then feel that "the friendship of the world is enmity with God?" and will he remember that the most unpopular man on earth, during his life, was "Jesus of Nazareth, whom they *crucified?*"

And to those for whom neither the applause of nations nor the wealth of the Indies have attraction sufficient to draw from duty, but who are gifted with ardent affections, and whose dearest and most importunate sin is to bestow love and worship, due only to the Creator, upon the creature — to them comes an opportunity of satisfying to the full the strong and craving affections, at a sacrifice of principle seemingly *so* trifling as not to subject them to the strictures of the most moral community, or exclude them from the communion of the most puritanical Christian church, but which the microscopic eye of a faithful conscience will detect and expose. Will the tempted then remember, that, if duty demand it, the right hand must be cut off, the right eye plucked out, *Isaac offered up?*

In all her former sorrows, Sybil Middleton had been simply a passive sufferer, bearing meekly the troubles which she could not avert, but exercising no moral agency, practising no self-denial, achieving no victory. True, the mild virtues of patience and resignation had been brought out, but these were natural to Sybil hitherto; she could not have been otherwise than resigned and patient under suffering. But now there came a far greater trial — a duty demanding not self-immolation only — oh, no! that would have been comparatively a light grief, a slight test — but the sacrifice of one dearer than self, the casting out of the object of the heart's fondest affections, the hurling down of the idol of the soul's highest worship. The struggle was long and fierce; nights of watching, days of tears, weeks of sorrow, passed before Sybil could turn a deaf ear to the solicitations of affection and of interest, and resolve to be true to her present conceptions of duty. At last she took a pen, and wrote to Mr. Livingston as follows:

"Mr. Livingston: I have decided. We must meet no more. We must write no more. Let an ocean of silence and distance freeze up between us. Let us die to each other.

"Sybil."

Not until this letter was sealed and sent, did Sybil realize that all indeed was over. She threw herself upon the lounge — she buried her head in the pillows, as if to shut out all sight and sound, writhing and quivering as though in the extremity of mortal anguish — then starting from her couch, and tossing her wild hair from her face, she walked the floor with nervous and irregular steps, wringing and twisting her pale fingers together; and when this passion had exhausted its victim, she lay in the apathy of despair, content with the silence, darkness, and repose of her chamber — dreading light, sound, or disturbance — scarcely wishing for a change, though that change might bring happiness. Alas! for the reward of an approving conscience; alas! for the triumph of a victory over temptation; alas! for the support of conscious rectitude. She felt none of these consolations now — *none*. It is not in the first moments of such a victory, the soul exhausted with its struggles and prostrate with its sufferings, that such comfort can be received. It is not at the instant that the right hand is cut off, that the right eye is plucked out, and the wounds are still smarting and bleeding, that one feels it to be "better" so. It is not at the moment in which the most cherished object of the affections, which has become entwined with every fibre of the heart, is first torn away, and the severed tendons are lacerated and bleeding, that they can clasp any support, or repose on any pillow. The time of strength and joy does come — and it comes in beauty, in glory, and in permanency; but it dawns gradually as the morning after a night of storms and darkness. Sybil gradually obtained composure, by degrees became interested in her daily avocations, and eventually grew happy, realising that happiness does not consist in the accomplishment of our dearest wishes, but in the cultivation and exercise of our virtues.

I have dwelt too long upon the trials of Sybil, trials which were all comprised in the passage of a few years, which were acutely felt only for a few weeks. She had received the attacks of some severe troubles, and sustained the shock of one terrible disappointment; yet, now that she has survived the snows of seventy winters, now that her form is bowed, and her hair is white with age and not with grief, you might look upon that calm face, and believe that grief had never convulsed it; upon that clear brow, and believe that care had never clouded it; into that serene eye, and think that tears had never dimmed it. And more — you may hear it often observed, that "Mrs. Middleton has a very young-looking face for her age;" and the reply, "Yes, very; but then, she has never had any trouble to make her look old" — and that is all *they* know about it, reader!

And the pastor! Livingston obtained a pastoral charge in the South. He became eminent as a theologian, a philanthropist, and a moral philosopher; yet people said that in his private life he was a cold, severe ascetic, proof against all tender impressions — a very woman-hater; and that was all *they* knew about it, reader!

Verily, "The true greatness of human life is almost altogether out of sight."

THE END.

☞ MRS. SOUTHWORTH'S NEW BOOK. ☜

SELF-MADE
OR, OUT OF THE DEPTHS,

Is now Complete in Book Form, in Two Volumes. Price $1.75 each, or $3.50 a set, and is issued under the names of

"ISHMAEL!" AND "SELF-RAISED."

MRS. E. D. E. N. SOUTHWORTH'S COMPLETE WORKS.

Complete in forty-three volumes, bound in morocco cloth, with a full gilt back, price $1.75 each; or $75.25 a set, each set in a neat box. The following are their names:

Ishmael; or, In the Depths—being "Self-Made."
Self-Raised; or, From the Depths, sequel to "Ishmael."
Mrs. Southworth's "Mother-in-Law; or, Married in Haste."
The Phantom Wedding; or, The Fall of the House of Flint.

The Fatal Secret.
Cruel as the Grave.
Tried For Her Life.
Fair Play.
The Lost Heiress.
How He Won Her.
The Maiden Widow.
Victor's Triumph.
The Family Doom.
A Beautiful Fiend.
The Bride's Fate.
Bride of Llewellyn.
The Changed Brides.
The Spectre Lover.
Prince of Darkness.
The Christmas Guest.
Fallen Pride.
The Fortune Seeker.
Retribution.
The Bridal Eve.

The Fatal Marriage.
Love's Labor Won.
The Deserted Wife.
A Noble Lord.
The Gipsy's Prophecy.
Lost Heir Linlithgow.
The Three Beauties.
Vivia; Secret of Power.
The Artist's Love.
Allworth Abbey.
The Two Sisters.
Discarded Daughter.
The Widow's Son.
Wife's Victory.
The Missing Bride.
Lady of the Isle.
The Haunted Homestead.
The Curse of Clifton.
India; Pearl of Pearl River.
Mystery of Dark Hollow.

☞ *Above Books are for sale by all Booksellers, or copies will be sent to any one, to any place, at once, post-paid, on remitting price to the publishers,*

T. B. PETERSON & BROTHERS,
306 Chestnut St., Philadelphia, Pa.

T. B. PETERSON AND BROTHERS' NEW BOOKS.

Booksellers, News Agents, and all others in want of good and fast-selling books will please send in their orders at once.

HENRY GREVILLE'S GREAT NOVELS.

Philomène's Marriages. With Author's Preface. *By Henry Gréville,* author of "Dosia," and "Marrying Off a Daughter."
Pretty Little Countess Zina. *By Henry Gréville,* author of "Dosia," "Savéli's Expiation," "Sonia," and "A Friend."
Dosia. *A Russian Story. By Henry Gréville,* author of "Marrying Off a Daughter," "Savéli's Expiation," and "Gabrielle."
Marrying Off a Daughter. *A Love Story. By Henry Gréville,* author of "Dosia," "Savéli's Expiation," and "Sonia."
Above are in paper cover, price 75 cents each, or in cloth, at $1.25 each.

Savéli's Expiation. A Powerful Novel. By Henry Gréville.
A Friend; or, "L'Ami." By Henry Gréville, author of "Dosia."
Sonia. A Love Story. By Henry Gréville, author of "Dosia."
Gabrielle; or, The House of Maurèze. By Henry Gréville.
Above are in paper cover, price 50 cents each, or in cloth, at $1.00 each.

MRS. BURNETT'S LOVE STORIES.

Kathleen. A Love Story. By Mrs. Frances Hodgson Burnett, author of "That Lass o' Lowrie's," "Theo," and "Pretty Polly Pemberton."
A Quiet Life. By Mrs. Frances Hodgson Burnett, author of "Theo."
Miss Crespigny. A Charming Love Story. By author of "Kathleen."
Theo. A Love Story. By author of "Kathleen," "Miss Crespigny," etc.
Pretty Polly Pemberton. By author of "Kathleen," "Theo," etc.
Above are in paper cover, price 50 cents each, or in cloth, at $1.00 each.

Jarl's Daughter and Other Tales. By Mrs. Burnett. Price 25 cents.
Lindsay's Luck. By Mrs. Frances Hodgson Burnett. Price 25 cents.

MRS. SOUTHWORTH'S LOVE STORIES.

Sybil Brotherton. A Novel. By Mrs. Emma D. E. N. Southworth.
The Red Hill Tragedy. By Mrs. Emma D. E. N. Southworth.
Above are in paper cover, price 50 cents each, or in cloth, at $1.00 each.

OCTAVE FEUILLET'S GREATEST WORKS.

The Count de Camors. *The Man of the Second Empire. By Octave Feuillet,* author of "The Amours of Phillippe." Price 75 cents in paper cover, or $1.25 in morocco cloth, black and gold.
The Amours of Phillippe; or, Phillippe's Love Affairs. By Octave Feuillet. Price 50 cents in paper, or $1.00 in cloth, black and gold.

☞ Above Books will be sent, postage paid, on receipt of Retail Price, by T. B. Peterson & Brothers, Philadelphia, Pa. (A)

T. B. PETERSON AND BROTHERS' PUBLICATIONS.

☞ Orders solicited from Booksellers, Librarians, News Agents, and all others in want of good and fast-selling books. ☜

MRS. EMMA D. E. N. SOUTHWORTH'S WORKS.

Complete in forty-three large duodecimo volumes, bound in morocco cloth, gilt back, price $1.75 each; or $75.25 a set, each set is put up in a neat box.

The Phantom Wedding; or, The Fall of the House of Flint,............			$1 75
Self-Raised; From the Depths..	$1 75	The Fatal Marriage,...............	1 75
Ishmael; or, In the Depths,.....	1 75	The Deserted Wife,...............	1 75
The Mother-in-Law,...............	1 75	The Fortune Seeker,...............	1 75
The Fatal Secret,...................	1 75	The Bridal Eve,...................	1 75
How He Won Her,...............	1 75	The Lost Heiress,.................	1 75
Fair Play,............................	1 75	The Two Sisters,..................	1 75
The Spectre Lover,...............	1 75	Lady of the Isle,..................	1 75
Victor's Triumph,.................	1 75	Prince of Darkness,...............	1 75
A Beautiful Fiend,...............	1 75	The Three Beauties,...............	1 75
The Artist's Love,................	1 75	Vivia; or the Secret of Power,	1 75
A Noble Lord,.....................	1 75	Love's Labor Won,...............	1 75
Lost Heir of Linlithgow,........	1 75	The Gipsy's Prophecy,...........	1 75
Tried for her Life,................	1 75	Retribution........................	1 75
Cruel as the Grave,...............	1 75	The Christmas Guest,............	1 75
The Maiden Widow,.............	1 75	Haunted Homestead,............	1 75
The Family Doom,...............	1 75	Wife's Victory,....................	1 75
The Bride's Fate,..................	1 75	Allworth Abbey,..................	1 75
The Changed Brides,............	1 75	India; Pearl of Pearl River,..	1 75
Fallen Pride,........................	1 75	Curse of Clifton,..................	1 75
The Widow's Son,................	1 75	Discarded Daughter,.............	1 75
The Bride of Llewellyn,........	1 75	The Mystery of Dark Hollow,..	1 75
The Missing Bride; or, Miriam, the Avenger,......................................			1 75

Above are each in cloth, or each one is in paper cover, at $1.50 each.

MRS. CAROLINE LEE HENTZ'S WORKS.

Green and Gold Edition. Complete in twelve volumes, in green morocco cloth, price $1.75 each; or $21.00 a set, each set is put up in a neat box.

Ernest Linwood,...................	$1 75	Love after Marriage,.............	$1 75
The Planter's Northern Bride,..	1 75	Eoline; or Magnolia Vale,.....	1 75
Courtship and Marriage.........	1 75	The Lost Daughter,...............	1 75
Rena; or, the Snow Bird,......	1 75	The Banished Son,...............	1 75
Marcus Warland,..................	1 75	Helen and Arthur,................	1 75
Linda; or, the Young Pilot of the Belle Creole,........................			1 75
Robert Graham; the Sequel to "Linda; or Pilot of Belle Creole,"...			1 75

Above are each in cloth, or each one is in paper cover, at $1.50 each.

☞Above Books will be sent, postage paid, on receipt of Retail Price, by T. B. Peterson & Brothers, Philadelphia, Pa. (1)

2 T. B. PETERSON & BROTHERS' PUBLICATIONS.

MRS. ANN S. STEPHENS' WORKS.

Complete in twenty-three large duodecimo volumes, bound in morocco cloth, gilt back, price $1.75 each; or $40.25 a set, each set is put up in a neat box.

Norston's Rest,.................................$1 75	The Soldiers' Orphans,............$1 75
Bertha's Engagement,............... 1 75	A Noble Woman,...................... 1 75
Bellehood and Bondage,.......... 1 75	Silent Struggles,...................... 1 75
The Old Countess,.................... 1 75	The Rejected Wife,................. 1 75
Lord Hope's Choice,................. 1 75	The Wife's Secret,.................. 1 75
The Reigning Belle,................... 1 75	Mary Derwent,....................... 1 75
Palaces and Prisons,................. 1 75	Fashion and Famine,............... 1 75
Married in Haste,...................... 1 75	The Curse of Gold,................. 1 75
Wives and Widows,................. 1 75	Mabel's Mistake,..................... 1 75
Ruby Gray's Strategy................ 1 75	The Old Homestead,............... 1 75
Doubly False,.... 1 75	The Heiress,.... 1 75	The Gold Brick,... 1 75

Above are each in cloth, or each one is in paper cover, at $1.50 each.

MRS. C. A. WARFIELD'S WORKS.

Complete in nine large duodecimo volumes, bound in morocco cloth, gilt back, price $1.75 each; or $15.75 a set, each set is put up in a neat box.

The Cardinal's Daughter,.......$1 75	Miriam's Memoirs,..................$1 75
Ferne Fleming,........................ 1 75	Monfort Hall,........................ 1 75
The Household of Bouverie,.... 1 75	Sea and Shore...................... 1 75
A Double Wedding................ 1 75	Hester Howard's Temptation,.. 1 75
Lady Ernestine; or, The Absent Lord of Rocheforte,............... 1 75

BEST COOK BOOKS PUBLISHED.

Every housekeeper should possess at least one of the following Cook Books, as they would save the price of it in a week's cooking.

The Queen of the Kitchen. Containing 1007 Old Maryland
   Family Receipts for Cooking,...Cloth, $1 75
Miss Leslie's New Cookery Book,......................................Cloth, 1 75
Mrs. Hale's New Cook Book,..Cloth, 1 75
Petersons' New Cook Book,..Cloth, 1 75
Widdifield's New Cook Book,..Cloth, 1 75
Mrs. Goodfellow's Cookery as it Should Be,.....................Cloth, 1 75
The National Cook Book. By a Practical Housewife,........Cloth, 1 75
The Young Wife's Cook Book..Cloth, 1 75
Miss Leslie's New Receipts for Cooking,............................Cloth, 1 75
Mrs. Hale's Receipts for the Million,...................................Cloth, 1 75
The Family Save-All. By author of "National Cook Book," Cloth, 1 75
Francatelli's Modern Cook. With the most approved methods of
   French, English, German, and Italian Cookery. With Sixty-two
   Illustrations. One volume of 600 pages, bound in morocco cloth, 5 00

☞ Above Books will be sent, postage paid, on receipt of Retail Price, by T. B. Peterson & Brothers, Philadelphia, Pa.

T. B. PETERSON & BROTHERS' PUBLICATIONS. 3

MISS ELIZA A. DUPUY'S WORKS.

Complete in fourteen large duodecimo volumes, bound in morocco cloth, gilt back, price $1.75 each; or $24.50 a set, each set is put up in a neat box.

A New Way to Win a Fortune $1 75 | Why Did He Marry Her?......$1 75
The Discarded Wife,............... 1 75 | Who Shall be Victor?............ 1 75
The Clandestine Marriage,...... 1 75 | The Mysterious Guest,.......... 1 75
The Hidden Sin,..................... 1 75 | Was He Guilty?.................... 1 75
The Dethroned Heiress,......... 1 75 | The Cancelled Will,.............. 1 75
The Gipsy's Warning,............. 1 75 | The Planter's Daughter,......... 1 75
All For Love,........................ 1 75 | Michael Rudolph,................. 1 75

Above are each in cloth, or each one is in paper cover, at $1.50 each.

DOESTICKS' WORKS.

Complete in four large duodecimo volumes, bound in cloth, gilt back, price $1.75 each; or $7.00 a set, each set is put up in a neat box.

Doesticks' Letters,.................$1 75 | The Elephant Club,..............$1 75
Plu-Ri-Bus-Tah,..................... 1 75 | Witches of New York,.......... 1 75

Above are each in cloth, or each one is in paper cover, at $1.50 each.

JAMES A. MAITLAND'S WORKS.

Complete in seven large duodecimo volumes, bound in cloth, gilt back, price $1.75 each; or $12.25 a set, each set is put up in a neat box.

The Watchman,....................$1 75 | Diary of an Old Doctor,.......$1 75
The Wanderer,...................... 1 75 | Sartaroe,............................. 1 75
The Lawyer's Story,............... 1 75 | The Three Cousins,.............. 1 75
The Old Patroon; or the Great Van Brock Property,...................... 1 75

Above are each in cloth, or each one is in paper cover, at $1.50 each.

T. ADOLPHUS TROLLOPE'S WORKS.

Complete in seven large duodecimo volumes, bound in cloth, gilt back, price $1.75 each; or $12.25 a set, each set is put up in a neat box.

The Sealed Packet,................$1 75 | Dream Numbers,.................$1 75
Garstang Grange,.................. 1 75 | Beppo, the Conscript,........... 1 75
Leonora Casaloni,... 1 75 | Gemma,........ 1 75 | Marietta,............ 1 75

Above are each in cloth, or each one is in paper cover, at $1.50 each.

FREDRIKA BREMER'S WORKS.

Complete in six large duodecimo volumes, bound in cloth, gilt back, price $1.75 each; or $10.50 a set, each set is put up in a neat box.

Father and Daughter,............$1 75 | The Neighbors,...................$1 75
The Four Sisters,................... 1 75 | The Home,.......................... 1 75

Above are each in cloth, or each one is in paper cover, at $1.50 each.
Life in the Old World. In two volumes, cloth, price,...................... 3 50

☞ Above Books will be sent postage paid, on receipt of Retail Price, by T. B. Peterson & Brothers, Philadelphia, Pa.

4 T. B. PETERSON & BROTHERS' PUBLICATIONS.

WILKIE COLLINS' BEST WORKS.

Basil; or, The Crossed Path..$1 50 | The Dead Secret. 12mo........$1 50
Above are each in one large duodecimo volume, bound in cloth.
The Dead Secret, 8vo............... 75 | The Queen's Revenge,............... 75
Basil; or, the Crossed Path,....... 75 | Miss or Mrs?.......................... 50
Hide and Seek,......................... 75 | Mad Monkton,....................... 50
After Dark,............................... 75 | Sights a-Foot,....................... 50
The Stolen Mask,........ 25 | The Yellow Mask,... 25 | Sister Rose,... 25
The above books are each issued in paper cover, in octavo form.

FRANK FORRESTER'S SPORTING BOOK.

Frank Forrester's Sporting Scenes and Characters. By Henry William Herbert. With Illustrations by Darley. Two vols., cloth,...$4 00

EMERSON BENNETT'S WORKS.

Complete in seven large duodecimo volumes, bound in cloth, gilt back, price $1.75 each; or $12.25 a set, each set is put up in a neat box.
The Border Rover,...............$1 75 | Bride of the Wilderness,........$1 75
Clara Moreland,..................... 1 75 | Ellen Norbury,...................... 1 75
The Orphan's Trials,.............. 1 75 | Kate Clarendon,..................... 1 75
Viola; or Adventures in the Far South-West,...................... 1 75
Above are each in cloth, or each one is in paper cover, at $1.50 each.
The Heiress of Bellefonte,...... 75 | The Pioneer's Daughter,........ 75

GREEN'S WORKS ON GAMBLING.

Complete in four large duodecimo volumes, bound in cloth, gilt back, price $1.75 each; or $7.00 a set, each set is put up in a neat box.
Gambling Exposed,...............$1 75 | Reformed Gambler,..............$1 75
The Gambler's Life,................ 1 75 | Secret Band of Brothers......... 1 75
Above are each in cloth, or each one is in paper cover, at $1.50 each.

DOW'S PATENT SERMONS.

Complete in four large duodecimo volumes, bound in cloth, gilt back, price $1.50 each; or $6.00 a set, each set is put up in a neat box.
Dow's Patent Sermons, 1st Series, cloth,.....................$1 50 | Dow's Patent Sermons, 3d Series, cloth,......................$1 50
Dow's Patent Sermons, 2d Series, cloth,..................... 1 50 | Dow's Patent Sermons, 4th Series, cloth,...................... 1 50
Above are each in cloth, or each one is in paper cover, at $1.00 each.

MISS BRADDON'S WORKS.

Aurora Floyd,........................ 75 | The Lawyer's Secret,............. 25
Aurora Floyd, cloth............... 1 00 | For Better, For Worse,.......... 75

☞ Above books will be sent, postage paid, on receipt of **Retail Price**, by T. B. Peterson & Brothers, Philadelphia, Pa.

ALEXANDER DUMAS' WORKS.

Count of Monte-Cristo,	$1 50	Memoirs of a Physician,	$1 00
Edmond Dantes,	75	Queen's Necklace,	1 00
The Three Guardsmen,	75	Six Years Later,	1 00
Twenty Years After,	75	Countess of Charny,	1 00
Bragelonne,	75	Andree de Taverney,	1 00
The Iron Mask,	1 00	The Chevalier,	1 00
Louise La Valliere,	1 00	Forty-five Guardsmen,	1 00
Diana of Meridor,	1 00	The Iron Hand,	1 00
Adventures of a Marquis,	1 00	The Conscript,	1 50
Love and Liberty, (1792-'93)	1 50	Countess of Monte-Cristo,	1 00
Camille; or, The Fate of a Coquette, (La Dame Aux Camelias,)			1 50

The above are each in paper cover, or in cloth, price $1.75 each.

The Mohicans of Paris,	75	Annette; or, Lady of Pearls,	75
The Horrors of Paris,	75	George; or, Isle of France,	50
The Fallen Angel,	75	Madame De Chamblay	50
Felina de Chambure,	75	The Black Tulip,	50
Sketches in France,	75	The Corsican Brothers,	50
Isabel of Bavaria,	75	The Count of Moret,	50
Twin Lieutenants,	75	The Marriage Verdict,	50
Man with Five Wives,	75	Buried Alive,	25

GEORGE W. M. REYNOLDS' WORKS.

Mysteries Court of London,	$1 00	Mary Price,	$1 00
Rose Foster,	1 50	Eustace Quentin,	1 00
Caroline of Brunswick,	1 00	Joseph Wilmot,	1 00
Venetia Trelawney,	1 00	Banker's Daughter,	1 00
Lord Saxondale,	1 00	Kenneth,	1 00
Count Christoval,	1 00	The Rye-House Plot,	1 00
Rosa Lambert,	1 00	The Necromancer,	1 00
Wallace, the Hero of Scotland,	1 00	The Gipsy Chief,	1 00
The Mysteries of the Court of Naples, full of Illustrations			1 00
Robert Bruce, the Hero-King of Scotland, full of Illustrations,			1 00

The above are each in paper cover, or in cloth, price $1.75 each.

Mary Stuart, Queen of Scots,	75	Ellen Percy,	75
The Opera Dancer,	75	Agnes Evelyn,	75
Child of Waterloo,	75	Pickwick Abroad,	75
Isabella Vincent,	75	Parricide,	75
Vivian Bertram,	75	Discarded Queen,	75
Countess of Lascelles,	75	Life in Paris,	50
Duke of Marchmont,	75	The Countess and the Page,	75
Massacre of Glencoe,	75	Edgar Montrose,	50
Loves of the Harem,	75	The Ruined Gamester,	50
The Soldier's Wife,	75	Clifford and the Actress,	50
May Middleton,	75	Ciprina; or, the Secrets,	50

☞ Above books will be sent, postage paid, on receipt of Retail Price, by T. B. Peterson & Brothers, Philadelphia, Pa.

CHARLES LEVER'S BEST WORKS.

Charles O'Malley,	75	Arthur O'Leary,	75
Harry Lorrequer,	75	Con Cregan,	75
Jack Hinton,	75	Davenport Dunn,	75
Tom Burke of Ours,	75	Horace Templeton,	75
Knight of Gwynne,	75	Kate O'Donoghue,	75

Above are in paper cover, or a fine edition is in cloth at $2.00 each.

A Rent in a Cloud,	50	St. Patrick's Eve,	50

Ten Thousand a Year, in one volume, paper cover, $1.50; or in cloth, 2 00
The Diary of a Medical Student, by author "Ten Thousand a Year," 75

MRS. HENRY WOOD'S BEST BOOKS.

The Master of Greylands,	$1 50	The Shadow of Ashlydyat,	$1 50
Within the Maze,	1 50	Squire Trevlyn's Heir,	1 50
Dene Hollow,	1 50	Oswald Cray,	1 50
Bessy Rane,	1 50	Mildred Arkell,	1 50
George Canterbury's Will,	1 50	The Red Court Farm,	1 50
Verner's Pride,	1 50	Elster's Folly,	1 50
The Channings,	1 50	Saint Martin's Eve,	1 50
Roland Yorke. A Sequel to "The Channings,"			1 50
Lord Oakburn's Daughters; or, The Earl's Heirs,			1 50
The Castle's Heir; or, Lady Adelaide's Oath,			1 50

The above are each in paper cover, or in cloth, price $1.75 each.

Edina; or, Missing Since Midnight, cloth, $1, paper cover,			75
The Mystery	75	A Life's Secret,	50
Parkwater. Told in Twilight,	75	The Haunted Tower,	50
The Lost Bank Note,	50	The Runaway Match,	25
The Lost Will,	50	Martyn Ware's Temptation,	25
Orville College,	50	The Dean of Denham,	25
Five Thousand a Year,	25	Foggy Night at Offord,	25
The Diamond Bracelet,	25	William Allair,	25
Clara Lake's Dream,	25	A Light and a Dark Christmas,	25
The Nobleman's Wife,	25	The Smuggler's Ghost	25
Frances Hildyard,	25	Rupert Hall,	25
Cyrilla Maude's First Love,	25	My Husband's First Love,	25
My Cousin Caroline's Wedding	25	Marrying Beneath Your Station	25

EUGENE SUE'S GREAT WORKS.

The Wandering Jew,	$1 50	First Love	50
The Mysteries of Paris,	1 50	Woman's Love,	50
Martin, the Foundling,	1 50	Female Bluebeard,	50
Above are in cloth at $2.00 each.		Man-of-War's-Man,	50
Life and Adventures of Raoul de Surville. A Tale of the Empire,			25

☞ Above Books will be sent, postage paid, on receipt of Retail Price, by T. B. Peterson & Brothers, Philadelphia, Pa.

NEW BOOKS BY THE VERY BEST AUTHORS.

The Shadow of Hampton Mead. A *Charming Story.* By *Mrs. Elizabeth Van Loon,* author of "A Heart Twice Won." One large duodecimo volume, in morocco cloth, black and gold. Price $1.50.

A Heart Twice Won; or, Second Love. *A Love Story.* By *Mrs. Elizabeth Van Loon,* author of "The Shadow of Hampton Mead," and in uniform style with it. Cloth, black and gold. Price $1.50.

Father Tom and the Pope; or, A Night at the Vatican. With Illustrative Engravings of the scenes that took place between the Pope and Father Tom. Paper cover, 50 cents, cloth, black and gold, $1.00.

EMILE ZOLA'S GREAT WORKS.

Hélène. *A Tale of Love, Passion and Remorse.* By *Emile Zola,* author of "The Abbé's Temptation," "L'Assommoir," etc. Price 75 cents in paper cover, or $1.25 in morocco cloth, black and gold.

The Abbé's Temptation. *A Love Story.* By *Emile Zola,* author of "Hélène." His Greatest Work. Price 75 cents in paper cover, or $1.25 in morocco cloth, black and gold.

WORKS BY THE VERY BEST AUTHORS.

The following books are each issued in one large duodecimo volume, bound in cloth, at $1.75 each, or each one is in paper cover, at $1.50 each.

The Initials. A Love Story. By Baroness Tautphœus,................$1 75
Married Beneath Him. By author of "Lost Sir Massingberd,"...... 1 75
Margaret Maitland. By Mrs. Oliphant, author of "Zaidee,".......... 1 75
Family Pride. By author of "Pique," "Family Secrets," etc......... 1 75
Self-Sacrifice. By author of "Margaret Maitland," etc............... 1 75
The Woman in Black. A Companion to the "Woman in White,"... 1 75
Rose Douglas. A Companion to "Family Pride," and "Self Sacrifice," 1 75
Family Secrets. A Companion to "Family Pride," and "Pique,"... 1 75
Popery Exposed. An Exposition of Popery as it was and is,......... 1 75
The Autobiography of Edward Wortley Montagu,...................... 1 75
The Forsaken Daughter. A Companion to "Linda,"................... 1 75
Love and Liberty. A Revolutionary Story. By Alexander Dumas, 1 75
The Morrisons. By Mrs. Margaret Hosmer,............................ 1 75
The Rich Husband. By author of "George Geith,"..................... 1 75
Woodburn Grange. A Novel. By William Howitt,...................... 1 75
The Lost Beauty. By a Noted Lady of the Spanish Court,............ 1 75
My Hero. By Mrs. Forrester. A Charming Love Story,.............. 1 75
The Quaker Soldier. A Revolutionary Romance. By Judge Jones,... 1 75
Memoirs of Vidocq, the French Detective. His Life and Adventures, 1 75
The Belle of Washington. With her Portrait. By Mrs. N. P. Lasselle, 1 75
High Life in Washington. A Life Picture. By Mrs. N. P. Lasselle, 1 75

Above books are each in cloth, or each one is in paper cover, at $1.50 each.

☞ Above Books will be sent, postage paid, on Receipt of Retail Price, by T. B. Peterson & Brothers, Philadelphia, Pa.

8 T. B. PETERSON & BROTHERS' PUBLICATIONS.

WORKS BY THE VERY BEST AUTHORS.

The following books are each issued in one large duodecimo volume, bound in cloth, at $1.75 each, or each one is in paper cover at $1.50 each.

The Count of Monte-Cristo. By Alexander Dumas. Illustrated,...$1 75
The Countess of Monte-Cristo. Paper cover, price $1.00; or cloth,.. 1 75
Camille; or, the Fate of a Coquette. By Alexander Dumas,.......... 1 75
Love and Money. By J. B. Jones, author of the "Rival Belles,"... 1 75
The Brother's Secret; or, the Count De Mara. By William Godwin, 1 75
The Lost Love. By Mrs. Oliphant, author of "Margaret Maitland," 1 75
The Roman Traitor. By Henry William Herbert. A Roman Story, 1 75
The Bohemians of London. By Edward M. Whitty,.................. 1 75
Wild Sports and Adventures in Africa. By Major W. C. Harris, 1 75
Courtship and Matrimony. By Robert Morris. With a Portrait,... 1 75
The Jealous Husband. By Annette Marie Maillard,................. 1 75
The Life, Writings, and Lectures of the late "Fanny Fern,"......... 1 75
The Life and Lectures of Lola Montez, with her portrait,............. 1 75
Wild Southern Scenes. By author of "Wild Western Scenes,"...... 1 75
Currer Lyle; or, the Autobiography of an Actress. By Louise Reeder. 1 75
The Cabin and Parlor. By J. Thornton Randolph. Illustrated,..... 1 75
The Little Beauty. A Love Story. By Mrs. Grey,.................. 1 75
Lizzie Glenn; or, the Trials of a Seamstress. By T. S. Arthur,..... 1 75
Lady Maud; or, the Wonder of Kingswood Chase. By Pierce Egan, 1 75
Wilfred Montressor; or, High Life in New York. Illustrated........ 1 75
The Old Stone Mansion. By C. J. Peterson, author "Kate Aylesford," 1 75
Kate Aylesford. By Chas. J. Peterson, author "Old Stone Mansion,". 1 75
Lorrimer Littlegood, by author "Harry Coverdale's Courtship,"..... 1 75
The Earl's Secret. A Love Story. By Miss Pardoe,................ 1 75
The Adopted Heir. By Miss Pardoe, author of "The Earl's Secret," 1 75
Coal, Coal Oil, and all other Minerals in the Earth. By Eli Bowen, 1 75
Secession, Coercion, and Civil War. By J. B. Jones,................ 1 75

Above books are each in cloth, or each one is in paper cover, at $1.50 each.

The Dead Secret. By Wilkie Collins, author of "The Crossed Path," 1 50
The Crossed Path; or Basil. By Wilkie Collins,.................... 1 50
Indiana. A Love Story. By George Sand, author of "Consuelo," 1 50
Jealousy; or, Teverino. By George Sand, author of "Consuelo," etc. 1 50
Six Nights with the Washingtonians, Illustrated. By T. S. Arthur, 3 50
Comstock's Elocution and Model Speaker. Intended for the use of
  Schools, Colleges, and for private Study, for the Promotion of
  Health, Cure of Stammering, and Defective Articulation. By
  Andrew Comstock and Philip Lawrence. With 236 Illustrations.. 2 00
The Lawrence Speaker. A Selection of Literary Gems in Poetry and
  Prose, designed for the use of Colleges, Schools, Seminaries, Literary
  Societies. By Philip Lawrence, Professor of Elocution. 600 pages.. 2 00

☞ Above Books will be sent, postage paid, on receipt of Retail Price, by T. B. Peterson & Brothers, Philadelphia, Pa.

PETERSONS' 'STERLING SERIES'
OF NEW AND GOOD BOOKS.
Are the Cheapest Novels in the World.
Price 75 Cents Each in Paper, or $1.00 Each in Cloth.

"PETERSONS' STERLING SERIES OF NEW AND GOOD BOOKS" are all issued unabridged and entire, in uniform style, and are printed from large type, in octavo form, price Seventy-five cents each In paper cover, with the edges cut open all around; or One Dollar each, bound in morocco cloth, black and gold, and is the most popular series of Books ever printed. The following works have already been issued in this series, and a new one will follow every two weeks in the same style, same size, and at the same low price

SALATHIEL; THE WANDERING JEW. By Rev. George Croly.
AURORA FLOYD. A Love Story. By Miss Braddon.
MARRYING FOR MONEY. A Love Story in Real Life.
THACKERAY'S IRISH SKETCH BOOK. With 38 Illustrations.
EDINA. A Love Story. By Mrs. Henry Wood.
CORINNE; OR, ITALY. By Madame De Stael.
CYRILLA. A Love Story. By author of "The Initials."
FLIRTATIONS IN AMERICA; or, HIGH LIFE IN NEW YORK.
THE COQUETTE. A Tale of Love and Pride.
CHARLES O'MALLEY, The Irish Dragoon. By Charles Lever.
THE FLIRT. By author of "The Gambler's Wife."
THE DEAD SECRET. By Wilkie Collins.
THE WIFE'S TRIALS. By Miss Pardoe.
THE MAN WITH FIVE WIVES. By Alexander Dumas.
HARRY LORREQUER. By Charles Lever.
PICKWICK ABROAD. Illustrated. By G. W. M. Reynolds.
FIRST AND TRUE LOVE. By George Sand.
THE MYSTERY. A Love Story. By Mrs. Henry Wood.
THE STEWARD. By author of "Valentine Vox."
BASIL; or, THE CROSSED PATH. By Wilkie Collins.
POPPING THE QUESTION. By author of "The Jilt."
THE JEALOUS WIFE. By Miss Julia Pardoe.
SYLVESTER SOUND. By author of "Valentine Vox."
THE CONFESSIONS OF A PRETTY WOMAN.
THE RIVAL BEAUTIES. By Miss Pardoe.
WHITEFRIARS; Or, The Days of Charles the Second.
WEBSTER AND HAYNE'S SPEECHES. Unabridged.

☞ *Above Books are for sale by all Booksellers, or copies will be sent to any one, to any place, at once, post-paid, on remitting price to the Publishers,*

T. B. PETERSON & BROTHERS,
306 Chestnut St., Philadelphia, Pa.

Henry Gréville's New Works.

Philomene's Marriages. From the French of "*Les Mariages de Philomène.*" By *Henry Gréville*, author of "Dosia," "Savéli's Expiation," etc.

The American edition of "PHILOMÈNE'S MARRIAGES," contains a Preface written by Henry Gréville, addressed to her American Readers, which is not in the French edition. *Translated in Paris, from Henry Gréville's manuscript, by Miss Helen Stanley.*

Pretty Little Countess Zina. By *Henry Gréville*, author of "Dosia," "Savéli's Expiation," "A Friend," etc. *Translated by Mary Neal Sherwood.*

"PRETTY LITTLE COUNTESS ZINA" is a careful study. Zina, the youthful Countess, bears a certain resemblance to Dosia—that bewitching creature—in her dainty wilfulness, while the ward and cousin, Vassalissa, is an entire new creation.

Dosia. A Russian Story. *Complete and Unabridged.* By *Henry Gréville*, author of "Savéli's Expiation," "Marrying Off a Daughter," "Sonia," etc.

"DOSIA" has been crowned by the French Academy as the Prize Novel of the year. It is a charming story of Russian society, and is crisp, fresh and pure; while its fascination is powerful and legitimate. It is written with a rare grace of style, is brilliant, pleasing and attractive. "DOSIA" is an exquisite creation, and is pure and fresh as a rose.

Marrying Off a Daughter. By *Henry Gréville*, author of "Dosia," "Savéli's Expiation," "Gabrielle," "A Friend," etc. *Translated by Mary Neal Sherwood.*

"MARRYING OFF A DAUGHTER" is gay, sparkling, and pervaded by a delicious tone of quiet humor, while the individuality of the characters is very marked. The mother travels all over Europe to find a desirable *parti* for her pretty daughter, who has a tolerable dowry, but alas! husband after husband slips through the meshes of the net woven by the mother. Suffice it to say, that the book will be read and enjoyed by thousands.

Above books are 75 Cents each in paper cover, or $1.25 in cloth, black and gold.

A Friend; or, L'Ami. A Story of Every-Day Life. By *Henry Gréville*, author of "Sonia," and "Savéli's Expiation." *Translated in Paris by Miss Helen Stanley.*

The story of "A FRIEND," is one of every-day life in Paris at the present day, and shows Henry Gréville's great talent and peculiar skill in the analysis of character. She draws her characters remarkably well, and this tender and touching picture of French home-life will touch many hearts, as it shows how the love of a true and good woman will meet with its reward and triumph at the last, in the value of true, enduring love.

Sonia. A Russian Story. By *Henry Gréville*, author of "Savéli's Expiation," "Marrying Off a Daughter," "Gabrielle," etc. *Translated by Mary Neal Sherwood.*

"SONIA," is charming and refined, and is a powerful, graceful, domestic story, displaying the author's imaginative style and play of fancy, and is charmingly and most beautifully told—giving one a very distinct idea of every-day home life in Russia.

Savéli's Expiation. By *Henry Gréville.* A dramatic and powerful novel, and a pure love story. *Translated from the French, by Mary Neal Sherwood.*

One of the most dramatic and most powerful novels ever published is "SAVÉLI'S EXPIATION," and although the character on which the plot rests is strongly drawn, it is not overdrawn, but is true to the times and situation. Powerful as it is, it is free from exaggeration, while a pathetic love story is presented for relief.

Gabrielle; or, The House of Maurèze. *Translated from the French of Henry Gréville*, the most popular writer in Europe at the present time.

"GABRIELLE; OR, THE HOUSE OF MAURÈZE," is a very touching story, most skilfully told, and follows the life of a girl whose title it bears; but if we were to tell any more of the plot it would be to tell the story, so we advise all persons to get the book, and read it.

Four last are 50 Cents each in paper cover, or $1.00 in cloth, black and gold.

☞ *Above Books are for sale by all Booksellers, or copies will be sent to any place, at once, per mail, post-paid, on remitting price to the publishers,*

T. B. PETERSON & BROTHERS,
306 Chestnut St., Philadelphia, Pa.

BEAUTIFUL SNOW.
AN ENTIRE NEW ILLUSTRATED EDITION.
Describing the Life of Woman in Five Pictures, from Original Drawings, by Edward L. Henry.

BEAUTIFUL SNOW, AND OTHER POEMS. By J. W. Watson, author of "The Outcast." *An Entire New Illustrated Edition, describing the life of Woman in Five Pictures, from original designs drawn by Edward L. Henry.* One volume, octavo, printed on tinted plate paper, and bound in green morocco cloth, with gilt top, gilt sides, and beveled boards, price Two Dollars; or bound in maroon morocco cloth, with full gilt sides, full gilt edges, full gilt back, and beveled boards, price Three Dollars.

☞ *Above Book is for sale by all Booksellers, or copies will be sent to any one, to any place, at once, post-paid, on remitting price to the publishers,*

T. B. PETERSON & BROTHERS,
306 Chestnut St., Philadelphia, Pa.

Émile Zola's Great Book.

HÉLÈNE

A LOVE EPISODE.
(UNE PAGE D'AMOUR.)

BY ÉMILE ZOLA.
AUTHOR OF "L'ASSOMMOIR," ETC., ETC.

TRANSLATED FROM THE FRENCH BY MARY NEAL SHERWOOD.

"ÉMILE ZOLA" is one of the four great authors in France of the present day, and there he is called the cleverest of the four. His novel, "L'ASSOMMOIR," to be issued in a few days by us, has already passed through fifty-eight editions in Paris, and this one, which is extremely interesting—indeed, exciting—just issued there, has already passed into its thirty-eighth edition. One of the most noted literary editors in New York writes as follows to Mrs. Sherwood: "I have just finished reading, and return to you by mail, your advance copy of 'ZOLA'S' extraordinary book, 'HÉLÈNE.' It is admirably written, and is full of powerful and life-like delineations of character, and in this respect surpasses any of his preceding publications, and you, with your skill, will have no difficulty in rendering it into pure English. By all means translate it at once, and your publishers will have the honor of introducing the cleverest book as well as a new and the greatest writer of the day to the American public." And in a letter just received by Mrs. Sherwood from one of the most celebrated critics in Paris, he says: "Why do you not translate 'ZOLA'S' new book, 'HÉLÈNE,' at once? It is the great sensation over here. The book is admirably written by a truly great artist, with a powerful realism and absorbing interest, and would be a splendid card for you to play, and would prove to be a great success in America. The characters and scenes of the story are well conceived and well executed, and it is impossible to deny the author's great skill, and every reader will acknowledge 'Zola's' great power in 'HÉLÈNE.' Besides the story, there are many pages devoted to rapturous descriptions of Paris at sunrise, at noonday, at sunset, and at night. Zola has made his name famous, and he will find plenty of readers for all he writes. His name alone will make any book sell."

Paper Cover, 75 Cents. Morocco Cloth, Gilt and Black, $1.25.

☞ *The above book is printed on tinted paper, and is issued in square 12mo. form, in uniform shape with "Theo," "Kathleen," "Miss Crespigny," "A Quiet Life," and "Pretty Polly Pemberton," by Mrs. Burnett, and is for sale by all Booksellers, or copies will be sent to any one, at once, post-paid, on remitting price to the Publishers,*

T. B. PETERSON & BROTHERS,
306 Chestnut Street, Philadelphia, Pa.

FATHER TOM AND THE POPE

OR,

A NIGHT AT THE VATICAN.

With Illustrative Engravings of the scenes that took place there, between the Pope and the Priest, Father Tom.

Read what S. J. Prime, Esq., the Editor of the New York Christian Observer, says of "Father Tom and the Pope," in that paper, editorially.

"FATHER TOM AND THE POPE.—There is a time to laugh. And we had it when we read this book, with the taking title of 'Father Tom and the Pope.' It is a broad satire on the faith and practice of Mother Rome: too broad perhaps for this country, where the Irish brogue, Irish humor, and Irish technical terms are not as readily caught as they are in the green isle for which the book was written.

"Father Tom goes to Rome; he is a Romish Priest from Ireland, and in Rome, his Holiness invites the celebrated champion of the Church to take 'pot look wid him.' At the table the Pope offers him various kinds of wine, but Father Tom, more accustomed to something stronger and warmer, complains of the drink, and greatly to the disgust of the Pope produces a bottle of the 'rale stuff' from his coat pocket. His Holiness rebukes him for bringing his own liquor when coming to dine with the prince of princes, but catching a whiff of the whiskey across the table, asks for the bottle, brings it to his blessed nose, and exclaims, 'Holy Virgin! but it has the divine smell!'

"After this the Pope and Father Tom have a good time generally; the Priest produces another bottle from another pocket; calls for the housekeeper to bring the 'matarials' to brew a punch; she comes; a comely damsel; and then occurs a scene that introduces as keen a satire on one of the dogmas of Rome as was ever made, for the particulars of which we advise all persons to buy and read the book."

Price 50 Cents in paper cover, or $1.00 in Morocco cloth, black and gold.

☞ *"Father Tom and the Pope," will be found for sale by all Booksellers, and on all Rail-Road Trains, or copies of it will be sent to any one, to any place, at once, post-paid, on remitting the price of the edition wished, in a letter, to the publishers,*

T. B. PETERSON & BROTHERS,
No. 306 Chestnut Street, Philadelphia, Pa.

PETERSONS' "DOLLAR SERIES"
OF GOOD NOVELS, ARE THE BEST, LARGEST, AND CHEAPEST BOOKS IN THE WORLD.

Price One Dollar Each, in Cloth, Black and Gold.

A WOMAN'S THOUGHTS ABOUT WOMEN. By Miss Mulock.
THE LOVER'S TRIALS. By Mrs. Mary A. Denison.
THE PRIDE OF LIFE. A Love Story. By Lady Jane Scott.
THE BEAUTIFUL WIDOW. By Mrs. Percy B. Shelley.
CORA BELMONT; or, The Sincere Lover.
TWO WAYS TO MATRIMONY; or, Is It Love, or, False Pride?
LOST SIR MASSINGBERD. James Payn's Best Book.
THE CLYFFARDS OF CLYFFE. By James Payn.
MY SON'S WIFE. By the Author of "Caste."
THE RIVAL BELLES; or, Life in Washington. By J. B. Jones.
THE REFUGEE. By the author of "Omoo," "Typee," etc.
OUT OF THE DEPTHS. The Story of a Woman's Life.
THE MATCHMAKER. A Society Novel. By Beatrice Reynolds.
AUNT PATTY'S SCRAP BAG. By Mrs. Caroline Lee Hentz.
THE STORY OF "ELIZABETH." By Miss Thackeray.
FLIRTATIONS IN FASHIONABLE LIFE. By Catharine Sinclair.
THE HEIRESS IN THE FAMILY. By Mrs. Mackenzie Daniels.
LOVE AND DUTY. A Love Story. By Mrs. Hubback.
THE COQUETTE; or, The Life and Letters of Eliza Wharton.
SELF-LOVE. A Book for Young Ladies and for Women.
THE DEVOTED BRIDE. By St. George Tucker, of Virginia.
THE MAN OF THE WORLD. By William North.
THE RECTOR'S WIFE; or, The Valley of a Hundred Fires.
THE QUEEN'S FAVORITE; or, The Price of a Crown.
COUNTRY QUARTERS. By the Countess of Blessington.
THE CAVALIER. A Novel. By G. P. R. James.
SARATOGA! AND THE FAMOUS SPRINGS. A Love Story.
COLLEY CIBBER'S LIFE OF EDWIN FORREST, with Portrait.
WOMAN'S WRONG. A Book for Women. By Mrs. Eiloart.
HAREM LIFE IN EGYPT AND CONSTANTINOPLE.
THE OLD PATROON; or, The Great Van Broek Property.
THE MACDERMOTS OF BALLYCLORAN. By Anthony Trollope.
A LONELY LIFE.   TREASON AT HOME.   PANOLA!

☞ For sale by all Booksellers and News Agents, and published by

T. B. PETERSON & BROTHERS, Philadelphia.

Henry Gréville's Greatest Novel.
PRETTY LITTLE COUNTESS ZINA.
A RUSSIAN STORY.
BY HENRY GRÉVILLE,
AUTHOR OF "DOSIA," "MARRYING OFF A DAUGHTER," "SAVÉLI'S EXPIATION," "SONIA," "A FRIEND," AND "GABRIELLE."

TRANSLATED FROM THE FRENCH BY MARY NEAL SHERWOOD.
Paper Cover, 75 Cents. Morocco Cloth, Gilt and Black, $1.25.

"PRETTY LITTLE COUNTESS ZINA" is a careful study of the Countess Koumiassine, who, in the most unconscious manner, continues to make all about her very wretched by her arbitrary rule and love of power. Zina, the daughter, and youthful Countess, bears a certain resemblance to Dosia—that bewitching creature—in her dainty wilfulness, while the ward and cousin, Vassalissa, is a new creation. Mrs. Sherwood has the talent, most rare in a translator, of placing herself fully *en rapport* with the authors with whom she deals. It is therefore unnecessary to say that her part of this most charming tale is thoroughly well done, while the publishers deserve immense credit for their exertions in making the American public familiar with the best French literature, and we wish them all possible success in their enterprise.—*Critic*

HENRY GREVILLE'S GREAT WORKS.

PRETTY LITTLE COUNTESS ZINA. *By Henry Gréville,* author of "Dosia," "Savéli's Expiation," and "Gabrielle." Price 75 cents in paper, or $1.25 in cloth.

DOSIA. *By Henry Gréville,* author of "Savéli's Expiation," "Marrying Off a Daughter," "Sonia," and "Gabrielle." Price 75 cents in paper, or $1.25 in cloth.

MARRYING OFF A DAUGHTER. *By Henry Gréville,* author of "Dosia," "Savéli's Expiation," "Sonia," and "Gabrielle." Price 75 cents in paper, or $1.25 in cloth.

SAVELI'S EXPIATION. *By Henry Gréville.* A dramatic and powerful novel of Russian life, and a pure, pathetic love story. Price 50 cts. in paper, or $1.00 in cloth.

SONIA. A Russian Story. *By Henry Gréville,* author of "Savéli's Expiation," "Dosia," and "Marrying Off a Daughter." Price 50 cents in paper, or $1.00 in cloth.

A FRIEND; or, L'AMIE. *By Henry Gréville,* author of "Savéli's Expiation," "Dosia," and "Marrying Off a Daughter." Price 50 cents in paper, or $1.00 in cloth.

GABRIELLE; or, THE HOUSE OF MAUREZE. *By Henry Gréville,* author of "Dosia," "A Friend," "Savéli's Expiation." Price 50 cts. in paper, or $1.00 in cloth.

☞ *The above Books are printed on tinted paper, and are issued in uniform style with "Theo," "Kathleen," "Miss Crespigny," "A Quiet Life," "Lindsay's Luck," and "Pretty Polly Pemberton," by Mrs. Burnett, and are for sale by all Booksellers, or copies will be sent to any one, at once, post-paid, on remitting price to the Publishers,*

T. B. PETERSON & BROTHERS, Philadelphia, Pa.

MRS. BURNETT'S CHARMING STORIES.

FOR SALE BY ALL BOOKSELLERS, AND PUBLISHED BY
T. B. PETERSON & BROTHERS, PHILADELPHIA.
BEING REPRINTED FROM "PETERSON'S MAGAZINE," FOR WHICH THEY WERE ALL ORIGINALLY WRITTEN.

☞ *The following Charming Stories were all written by Mrs. Frances Hodgson Burnett, and each one is printed on tinted paper, the whole being issued in uniform shape and style, in square 12mo. form, being seven of the best, most interesting, and choicest love stories ever written.*

"THEO." A Love Story. By Mrs. Frances Hodgson Burnett, author of "Kathleen," "Pretty Polly Pemberton," "Miss Crespigny," "A Quiet Life," and "Lindsay's Luck."

KATHLEEN. A Love Story. By Mrs. Frances Hodgson Burnett, author of "Theo," "Miss Crespigny," "Jarl's Daughter," "A Quiet Life," and "Pretty Polly Pemberton."

A QUIET LIFE; and THE TIDE ON THE MOANING BAR. By Mrs. Frances Hodgson Burnett, author of "Theo."

MISS CRESPIGNY. A Powerful Love Story. By Mrs. Frances Hodgson Burnett, author of "Theo," "Kathleen," etc.

PRETTY POLLY PEMBERTON. A Charming Love Story. By Mrs. Frances Hodgson Burnett, author of "Kathleen."

Above are 50 Cents each in paper cover, or $1.00 each in cloth, black and gold.

JARL'S DAUGHTER; and OTHER STORIES. By Mrs. Frances Hodgson Burnett, author of "Theo," "Kathleen," etc.

LINDSAY'S LUCK. A Love Story. By Mrs. Frances Hodgson Burnett, author of "Theo," "Kathleen," "A Quiet Life," etc.

Above are each in one volume, paper cover, price 25 Cents each.

☞ *Above Books are for sale by all Booksellers and News Agents, or copies of any one or all of them, will be sent to any place, at once, per mail, post-paid, on remitting price to the Publishers,*

T. B. PETERSON & BROTHERS,
306 Chestnut Street, Philadelphia, Pa.

NEW AND POPULAR BOOKS

BY THE BEST AUTHORS, FOR SALE BY ALL BOOKSELLERS, AND PUBLISHED BY

T. B. PETERSON & BROTHERS, PHILADELPHIA.

PHILOMENE'S MARRIAGES. With a Preface by the Author. *By Henry Gréville*, author of "Dosia." Price 75 cents in paper cover, or $1.25 in cloth.

PRETTY LITTLE COUNTESS ZINA. *By Henry Gréville*, author of "Dosia," and "Savéli's Expiation." Price 75 cents in paper cover, or $1.25 in cloth.

JARL'S DAUGHTER; AND OTHER TALES. *By Mrs. Frances Hodgson Burnett*, author of "Theo," "Kathleen," and "Miss Crespigny." Paper cover, price 25 cents.

LINDSAY'S LUCK. *A Love Story. By Mrs. Frances Hodgson Burnett*, author of "Theo," "Kathleen," and "Pretty Polly Pemberton." Paper cover, price 25 cents.

FATHER TOM AND THE POPE; or, A NIGHT AT THE VATICAN. With Illustrations of scenes between the Pope and Father Tom. Paper, 50 cents, cloth, $1.00.

THE COUNT DE CAMORS. *The Man of the Second Empire. By Octave Feuillet*, author of "Amours of Phillippe." Price 75 cents in paper cover, or $1.25 in cloth.

SYBIL BROTHERTON. *By Mrs. E. D. E. N. Southworth*, author of "Ishmael," "Self-Raised," etc. Price 50 cents in paper cover, or $1.00 in cloth, black and gold.

THE ABBE'S TEMPTATION. *A Love Story. By Emile Zola*, author of "Héléne." His Greatest Work. Price 75 cents in paper cover, or $1.25 in cloth, black and gold.

THE SWAMP DOCTOR'S ADVENTURES IN THE SOUTH-WEST. With Fourteen Illustrations by Darley. Morocco cloth, gilt and black. Price $1.50.

THE SHADOW OF HAMPTON MEAD. *A Charming Story. By Elizabeth Van Loon*, author of "A Heart Twice Won." Cloth, black and gold. Price $1.50.

A HEART TWICE WON; or, SECOND LOVE. *By Mrs. Elizabeth Van Loon*, author of "The Shadow of Hampton Mead." Cloth, black and gold. Price $1.50.

HELENE. *A Tale of Love, Passion and Remorse. By Emile Zola*, author of "The Abbé's Temptation." Price 75 cents in paper cover, or $1.25 in cloth.

MADELEINE. *A Charming Love Story. By Jules Sandeau.* Crowned by the French Academy. Uniform with "Dosia." Paper cover. Price 50 cents.

DOSIA. *A Russian Story. By Henry Gréville*, author of "Marrying Off a Daughter," "Savéli's Expiation," and "Gabrielle." Price 75 cents in paper, or $1.25 in cloth.

MARRYING OFF A DAUGHTER. *A Love Story. By Henry Gréville*, author of "Dosia," and "Savéli's Expiation." Price 75 cents in paper, or $1.25 in cloth.

CARMEN. *By Prosper Mérimee, from which the opera of "Carmen" was dramatized.* Uniform with "Kathleen," etc. Price 50 cents in paper, or $1.00 in cloth.

COLONEL THORPE'S SCENES IN ARKANSAW. With Sixteen Illustrations, from Original Designs by Darley. Morocco cloth, gilt and black. Price $1.50.

FANCHON, THE CRICKET; or, LA PETITE FADETTE. *By George Sand.* This is the original work from which the play of "Fanchon, the Cricket," as presented on the stage, was dramatized. Price 50 cents in paper cover, or a finer edition, in a larger duodecimo volume, bound in morocco cloth, black and gold, price $1.50.

☞ Above Books are for sale by all Booksellers and News Agents, or copies of any one or more, will be sent to any place, post-paid, on remitting price to the publishers,

T. B. PETERSON & BROTHERS, Philadelphia, Pa.

NEW AND POPULAR BOOKS

☞ *The following New Books are printed on tinted paper, and are issued in uniform style, in square 12mo. form. Price Fifty Cents each in Paper Cover, or One Dollar each in Morocco Cloth, Black and Gold. They are the most charming Novels ever printed.*

KATHLEEN. A Love Story. *By Mrs. Frances Hodgson Burnett,* author of "Theo," "Miss Crespigny," and "Pretty Polly Pemberton," etc.

"THEO." A Love Story. *By Mrs. Frances Hodgson Burnett,* author of "Kathleen," "Pretty Polly Pemberton," "Miss Crespigny," "A Quiet Life," etc.

PRETTY POLLY PEMBERTON. A Powerful Love Story. *By Mrs. Frances Hodgson Burnett,* author of "Theo," "Kathleen," and "Miss Crespigny."

MISS CRESPIGNY. A Charming Love Story. *By Mrs. Frances Hodgson Burnett,* author of "Theo," "Kathleen," "Jarl's Daughter," and "A Quiet Life."

A QUIET LIFE. *By Mrs. Frances Hodgson Burnett,* author of "Theo," "Kathleen," "Pretty Polly Pemberton," "Miss Crespigny," "Jarl's Daughter," etc.

A FRIEND; or, L'AMI. *By Henry Gréville,* author of "Sonia," "Savéli's Expiation," and "Marrying Off a Daughter." *Translated by Miss Helen Stanley.*

SONIA. A Russian Story. *By Henry Gréville,* author of "Marrying Off a Daughter," "Savéli's Expiation," "Gabrielle." *Translated by Mary Neal Sherwood.*

SAVELI'S EXPIATION. *By Henry Gréville.* A dramatic and powerful novel of Russian life, and a pure, pathetic love story. *Translated by Mary Neal Sherwood.*

GABRIELLE; or, THE HOUSE OF MAUREZE. *By Henry Gréville,* author of "Savéli's Expiation," "Dosia," "Marrying Off a Daughter," etc.

A WOMAN'S MISTAKE; or, JACQUES DE TREVANNES. A Charming Love Story. *From the French of Madame Angèle Dussaud, by Mary Neal Sherwood.*

MADAME POMPADOUR'S GARTER; or, THE DAYS OF MADAME POMPADOUR. A Romance of the Reign of Louis XV. *By Gabrielle De St. Andre.*

THE MATCHMAKER. A Charming Novel. *By Beatrice Reynolds.* All the characters and scenes in it have all the freshness of life, and all the vitality of truth.

TWO WAYS TO MATRIMONY; or, IS IT LOVE? or, FALSE PRIDE. A book for Ladies and Gentlemen; for Parents, and for all those contemplating Matrimony.

THAT GIRL OF MINE. A Love Story. By the author of *"That Lover of Mine."* It is one of the most brilliant novels of Washington City society ever issued.

THE RED HILL TRAGEDY. A Novel. *By Mrs. Emma D. E. N. Southworth,* author of "Ishmael," "Self-Raised," "The Mother-in-Law," etc.

THE AMOURS OF PHILLIPPE. A History of "PHILLIPPE'S LOVE AFFAIRS." *By Octave Feuillet,* author of "The Count de Camors, the Man of the Second Empire."

BESSIE'S SIX LOVERS. A Charming Love Story, of the purest and best kind.

THAT LOVER OF MINE. A Love Story. By author of *"That Girl of Mine."*

STORY OF "ELIZABETH." By Miss Thackeray, daughter of W. M. Thackeray.

Above Books are 50 Cents each in Paper Cover, or $1.00 each in Cloth.

☞ *Above Books are for sale by all Booksellers and News Agents, or copies of any one or more, will be sent to any place, post-paid, on remitting price to the publishers,*

T. B. PETERSON & BROTHERS, Philadelphia, Pa.

ALEXANDER DUMAS' GREAT WORKS.

All or any will be sent free of postage, everywhere, to all, on receipt of remittances.

The Count of Monte-Cristo. With elegant illustrations, and portraits of Edmond Dantes, Mercedes, and Fernand. Price $1.50 in paper cover; or $1.75 in cloth.
Edmond Dantes. A Sequel to the "Count of Monte-Cristo." In one large octavo volume. Price 75 cents in paper cover, or a finer edition, bound in cloth, for $1.75.
The Countess of Monte-Cristo. With a portrait of the "Countess of Monte-Cristo" on the cover. One large octavo volume, paper cover, price $1.00; or bound in cloth, for $1.75.
The Three Guardsmen; or, The Three Mousquetaires. In one large octavo volume. Price 75 cents in paper cover, or a finer edition in cloth, for $1.75.
Twenty Years After. A Sequel to the "Three Guardsmen." In one large octavo volume. Price 75 cents in paper cover, or a finer edition, in one volume, cloth, for $1.75.
Bragelonne; the Son of Athos. Being the continuation of "Twenty Years After." In one large octavo volume. Price 75 cents in paper cover, or a finer edition in cloth, for $1.75.
The Iron Mask. Being the continuation of the "Three Guardsmen," "Twenty Years After," and "Bragelonne." In one large octavo volume. Paper cover, $1.00; or in cloth, for $1.75.
Louise La Valliere; or, the Second Series of the "Iron Mask," and end of "The Three Guardsmen" series. In one large octavo volume. Paper cover, $1.00; or in cloth, for $1.75.
The Memoirs of a Physician; or, The Secret History of the Court of Louis the Fifteenth. Beautifully Illustrated. In one large octavo volume. Paper cover, $1.00; or in cloth, for $1.75.
The Queen's Necklace; or, The "Second Series of the Memoirs of a Physician." In one large octavo volume. Paper cover, price $1.00; or in one volume, cloth, for $1.75.
Six Years Later; or, Taking of the Bastile. Being the "Third Series of the Memoirs of a Physician." In one large octavo volume. Paper cover, $1.00; or in cloth, for $1.75.
Countess of Charny; or, The Fall of the French Monarchy. Being the "Fourth Series of the Memoirs of a Physician." In one large octavo volume. Paper cover, $1.00; or in cloth, for $1.75.
Andree de Taverney. Being the "Fifth Series of the Memoirs of a Physician." In one large octavo volume. Paper cover, price $1.00; or in one volume, cloth, for $1.75.
The Chevalier; or, the "Sixth Series and final conclusion of the Memoirs of a Physician Series." In one large octavo volume. Price $1.00 in paper cover; or $1.75 in cloth.
Joseph Balsamo. Dumas' greatest work, from which the play of "Joseph Balsamo" was dramatized, by his son, Alexander Dumas, Jr. Price $1.00 in paper cover, or $1.50 in cloth.
The Conscript; or, The Days of the First Napoleon. An Historical Novel. In one large duodecimo volume. Price $1.50 in paper cover; or in cloth, for $1.75.
Camille; or, The Fate of a Coquette. ("La Dame aux Camelias.") This is the only true and complete translation of "Camille," and it is from this translation that the Play of "Camille," and the Opera of "La Traviata" was adapted to the Stage. Paper cover, price $1.50; or in cloth, $1.75.
Love and Liberty; or, A Man of the People. (Rene Besson.) A Thrilling Story of the French Revolution of 1792-93. In one large duodecimo volume, paper cover, $1.50; cloth, $1.75.
The Adventures of a Marquis. Paper cover, $1.00; or in one volume, cloth, for $1.75.
The Forty-Five Guardsmen. Paper cover, $1.00; or in one volume, cloth, for $1.75.
Diana of Meridor. Paper cover, $1.00; or in one volume, cloth, for $1.75.
The Iron Hand. Price $1.00 in paper cover, or in one volume, cloth, for $1.75.
Isabel of Bavaria, Queen of France. In one large octavo volume. Price 75 cents.
Annette; or, The Lady of the Pearls. A Companion to "Camille." Price 75 cents.
The Fallen Angel. A Story of Love and Life in Paris. One large volume. Price 75 cents.
The Mohicans of Paris. In one large octavo volume. Price 75 cents.
The Horrors of Paris. In one large octavo volume. Price 75 cents.
The Man with Five Wives. In one large octavo volume. Price 75 cents.
Sketches in France. In one large octavo volume. Price 75 cents.
Felina de Chambure; or, The Female Fiend. Price 75 cents.
The Twin Lieutenants; or, The Soldier's Bride. Price 75 cents.
Madame de Chamblay. In one large octavo volume. Price 50 cents.
The Black Tulip. In one large octavo volume. Price 50 cents.
The Corsican Brothers. In one large octavo volume. Price 50 cents.
George; or, The Planter of the Isle of France. Price 50 cents.
The Count of Moret. In one large octavo volume. Price 50 cents.
The Marriage Verdict. In one large octavo volume. Price 50 cents.
Buried Alive. In one large octavo volume. Price 25 cents.

☞ *Above books are for sale by all Booksellers and News Agents, or copies of any one or more, will be sent to any one, post-paid, on remitting price to the Publishers,*

T. B. PETERSON & BROTHERS, Philadelphia, Pa.

GEORGE W. M. REYNOLDS' WORKS.
NEW AND BEAUTIFUL EDITIONS, JUST READY.
Each Work is complete and unabridged, in one large volume.
All or any will be sent free of postage, everywhere, to all, on receipt of remittances.

Mysteries of the Court of London; being THE MYSTERIES OF THE COURT OF GEORGE THE THIRD, with the Life and Times of the PRINCE OF WALES, afterward GEORGE THE FOURTH. Complete in one large volume, bound in cloth, price $1.75; or in paper cover, price $1.00.
Rose Foster; or, the "Second Series of the Mysteries of the Court of London." Complete in one large volume, bound in cloth, price $1.75; or in paper cover, price $1.50.
Caroline of Brunswick; or, the "Third Series of the Mysteries of the Court of London." Complete in one large volume, bound in cloth, price $1.75; or in paper cover, price $1.00.
Venetia Trelawney; being the "Fourth Series or final conclusion of the Mysteries of the Court of London." Complete in one large volume, bound in cloth, price $1.75; or in paper cover, price $1.00.
Lord Saxondale; or, The Court of Queen Victoria. Complete in one large volume, bound in cloth, price $1.75; or in paper cover, price $1.00.
Count Christoval. The "Sequel to Lord Saxondale." Complete in one large volume, bound in cloth, price $1.75; or in paper cover, price $1.00.
Rosa Lambert; or, The Memoirs of an Unfortunate Woman. Complete in one large volume, bound in cloth, price $1.75; or in paper cover, price $1.00.
Joseph Wilmot; or, The Memoirs of a Man Servant. Complete in one large volume, bound in cloth, price $1.75; or in paper cover, price $1.00.
The Banker's Daughter. A Sequel to "Joseph Wilmot." Complete in one large volume, bound in cloth, price $1.75; or in paper cover, price $1.00.
The Rye-House Plot; or, Ruth, the Conspirator's Daughter. Complete in one large volume, bound in cloth, price $1.75; or in paper cover, price $1.00.
The Necromancer. Being the Mysteries of the Court of Henry the Eighth. Complete in one large volume, bound in cloth, price $1.75; or in paper cover, price $1.00.
Mary Price; or, The Adventures of a Servant Maid. One vol., cloth, price $1.75; or in paper, $1.00.
Eustace Quentin. A "Sequel to Mary Price." One vol., cloth, price $1.75; or in paper, $1.00.
The Mysteries of the Court of Naples. Price $1.00 in paper cover; or $1.75 in cloth.
Kenneth. A Romance of the Highlands. One vol., cloth, price $1.75; or in paper cover, $1.00.
Wallace: the Hero of Scotland. Illustrated with 38 plates. Paper, $1.00; cloth, $1.75.
The Gipsy Chief. Beautifully Illustrated. Price $1.00 in paper cover, or $1.75 in cloth.
Robert Bruce; the Hero King of Scotland. Illustrated. Paper, $1.00; cloth, $1.75.
The Opera Dancer; or, The Mysteries of London Life. Price 75 cents.
Isabella Vincent; or, The Two Orphans. One large octavo volume. Price 75 cents.
Vivian Bertram; or, A Wife's Honor. A Sequel to "Isabella Vincent." Price 75 cents.
The Countess of Lascelles. The Continuation to "Vivian Bertram." Price 75 cents.
Duke of Marchmont. Being the Conclusion of "The Countess of Lascelles." Price 75 cents.
The Child of Waterloo; or, The Horrors of the Battle Field. Price 75 cents.
Pickwick Abroad. A Companion to the "Pickwick Papers," by "Boz." Price 75 cents.
The Countess and the Page. One large octavo volume. Price 75 cents.
Mary Stuart, Queen of Scots. Complete in one large octavo volume. Price 75 cents.
The Soldier's Wife. Illustrated. One large octavo volume. Price 75 cents.
May Middleton; or, The History of a Fortune. In one large octavo volume. Price 75 cents.
The Loves of the Harem. One large octavo volume. Price 75 cents.
Ellen Percy; or, The Memoirs of an Actress. One large octavo volume. Price 75 cents.
The Discarded Queen. One large octavo volume. Price 75 cents.
Agnes Evelyn; or, Beauty and Pleasure. One large octavo volume. Price 75 cents.
The Massacre of Glencoe. One large octavo volume. Price 75 cents.
The Parricide; or, Youth's Career in Crime. Beautifully Illustrated. Price 75 cents.
Ciprina; or, The Secrets of a Picture Gallery. One volume. Price 50 cents.
The Ruined Gamester. With Illustrations. One large octavo volume. Price 50 cents.
Life in Paris. Handsomely illustrated. One large octavo volume. Price 50 cents.
Clifford and the Actress. One large octavo volume. Price 50 cents.
Edgar Montrose. One large octavo volume. Price 50 cents.

☞ *The above works will be found for sale by all Booksellers and News Agents.*
☞ *Copies of any one, or more, or all of Reynolds' works, will be sent to any place, at once, post-paid, on remitting price of ones wanted to the Publishers,*

T. B. PETERSON & BROTHERS, Philadelphia, Pa.

"It is worth double its price."—*Ottawa, (Canada), Advertiser.*

☞CHEAPEST AND BEST!☜
PETERSON'S MAGAZINE
☞FULL-SIZE PAPER PATTERNS!☜

☞ A SUPPLEMENT *will be given in every number for 1879, containing a full-size pattern sheet for a lady's, or child's dress. Every subscriber will receive, during the year, twelve of these patterns, so that these alone will be worth more than the subscription price. Great improvements will also be made in other respects.*☜

"PETERSON'S MAGAZINE" contains, every year, 1000 pages, 14 steel plates, 12 colored Berlin patterns, 12 mammoth colored fashion plates, 24 pages of music, and about 900 wood cuts. Its principal embellishments are

SUPERB STEEL ENGRAVINGS!

Its immense circulation enables its proprietor to spend more on embellishments, stories, &c. than any other. It gives more for the money, and combines more merits, than any in the world. Its

THRILLING TALES AND NOVELETTES

Are the best published anywhere. All the most popular writers are employed to write originally for "*Peterson.*" In 1879, in addition to the usual quantity of short stories, FIVE ORIGINAL COPYRIGHT NOVELETTES will be given, by Ann S. Stephens, Frank Lee Benedict, Frances Hodgson Burnett, Jane G. Austin, and that unrivalled humorist, the author of "Josiah Allen's Wife."

MAMMOTH COLORED FASHION PLATES

Ahead of all others. These plates are engraved on steel, twice the usual size, and are unequalled for beauty. They will be superbly colored. Also, Household and other receipts; articles on "Wax-Work Flowers," "Management of Infants;" in short everything interesting to ladies.
N. B.—As the publishers now prepay the postage to all mail subscribers, "*Peterson*" is CHEAPER THAN EVER; *in fact is* THE CHEAPEST IN THE WORLD.

TERMS (Always in Advance) $2.00 A YEAR.
☞REDUCED PRICES TO CLUBS☜

2 Copies for $3.50
3   "   "   4.50   { With a copy of the premium picture (24 x 20) "CHRIST BLESSING LITTLE CHILDREN," *a five dollar engraving,* to the person getting up the Club.

4 Copies for $6.50
6   "   "   9.00   { With an extra copy of the Magazine for 1879, as a premium, to the person getting up the Club.

5 Copies for $8.00
7   "   " 10.50   { With both an extra copy of the Magazine for 1879, and the premium picture, *a five dollar engraving,* to the person getting up the Club.

Address, post-paid,

CHARLES J. PETERSON,
300 Chestnut St., Philadelphia, Pa.

☞ Specimens sent gratis if written for.

Mrs. Southworth's Works.

EACH IS IN ONE LARGE DUODECIMO VOLUME, MOROCCO CLOTH, GILT BACK, PRICE $1.75 EACH.

All or any will be sent free of postage, everywhere, to all, on receipt of remittances.

ISHMAEL; or, IN THE DEPTHS. (Being "Self-Made; or, Out of Depths.")
SELF-RAISED; or, From the Depths. The Sequel to "Ishmael."
THE PHANTOM WEDDING; or, the Fall of the House of Flint.
THE "MOTHER-IN-LAW;" or, MARRIED IN HASTE.
THE MISSING BRIDE; or, MIRIAM, THE AVENGER.
VICTOR'S TRIUMPH. The Sequel to "A Beautiful Fiend."
A BEAUTIFUL FIEND; or, THROUGH THE FIRE.
THE LADY OF THE ISLE; or, THE ISLAND PRINCESS.
FAIR PLAY; or, BRITOMARTE, THE MAN-HATER.
HOW HE WON HER. The Sequel to "Fair Play."
THE CHANGED BRIDES; or, Winning Her Way.
THE BRIDE'S FATE. The Sequel to "The Changed Brides."
CRUEL AS THE GRAVE; or, Hallow Eve Mystery.
TRIED FOR HER LIFE. The Sequel to "Cruel as the Grave."
THE CHRISTMAS GUEST; or, The Crime and the Curse.
THE LOST HEIR OF LINLITHGOW; or, The Brothers.
A NOBLE LORD. The Sequel to "The Lost Heir of Linlithgow."
THE FAMILY DOOM; or, THE SIN OF A COUNTESS.
THE MAIDEN WIDOW. The Sequel to "The Family Doom."
THE GIPSY'S PROPHECY; or, The Bride of an Evening.
THE FORTUNE SEEKER; or, Astrea, The Bridal Day.
THE THREE BEAUTIES; or, SHANNONDALE.
FALLEN PRIDE; or, THE MOUNTAIN GIRL'S LOVE.
THE DISCARDED DAUGHTER; or, The Children of the Isle.
THE PRINCE OF DARKNESS; or, HICKORY HALL.
THE TWO SISTERS; or, Virginia and Magdalene.
THE FATAL MARRIAGE; or, ORVILLE DEVILLE.
INDIA; or, THE PEARL OF PEARL RIVER.   THE CURSE OF CLIFTON.
THE WIDOW'S SON; or, LEFT ALONE.   THE WIFE'S VICTORY.
THE MYSTERY OF DARK HOLLOW.   THE SPECTRE LOVER.
ALLWORTH ABBEY; or, EUDORA.   THE ARTIST'S LOVE.
THE BRIDAL EVE; or, ROSE ELMER.   THE FATAL SECRET.
VIVIA; or, THE SECRET OF POWER.   LOVE'S LABOR WON.
THE HAUNTED HOMESTEAD.   THE LOST HEIRESS.
BRIDE OF LLEWELLYN.   THE DESERTED WIFE.   RETRIBUTION.

☞ Mrs. Southworth's works will be found for sale by all Booksellers.
☞ Copies of any one, or more of Mrs. Southworth's works, will be sent to any place, at once, per mail, post-paid, on remitting price of ones wanted to the Publishers,

T. B. PETERSON & BROTHERS, Philadelphia, Pa.

www.ingramcontent.com/pod-product-compliance
Lightning Source LLC
Chambersburg PA
CBHW032157160426
43197CB00008B/956